Praise for
Global Inspirations

In *Global Inspirations*, Michael has gifted us with his inspiring accounts of how God carried out His amazing plans after changing the course of this civil engineer's life. Not only does Michael help us to visualize the various places in the world where he served, but especially he leads us to see how God works among His people and carries out His purposes, even in dire and devastating circumstances.

– Pastor Michel, Peace Lutheran Church, New Berlin, WI

Michael's faith pilgrimage expresses the extraordinary story of God found in the experience of being one of the countless ordinary apostles, bearing love exactly where God desires. My hope is that Michael's story may also encourage others to reflect on their own story with God and how God is working through them in grace and love, and then also share the story with others.

– Rev'd Dr. Christian D. Boyd, Pastor, Southminster Presbyterian Church (U.S.A.)

Michael's humility, faith and generosity of heart are evident on every page: he comes to love, admire and learn from the people he meets wherever he goes about the nature of authentic faith, hope and love, the importance of courage, perseverance and community, the beauty of healing and the power of a stranger's smile. This book is truly a global inspiration, an invitation to us all to learn from "the least of these" whom God so loves.

– Deborah Smith Douglas, author of *The Praying Life: Seeing God in All Things*

My father, Paul Johnson, is one of the mentors mentioned by Michael in his book and had nothing but praise for Michael's engineering skills and his passion to serve others—they were cut from the same cloth. It was heartwarming to learn how people who had so little and who faced destruction in their lives trusted in the Lord—and that this in turn inspired Michael's own faith. Michael's stories in *Global Inspirations* are a testament to someone living out the directive from the apostle Peter that "each of you should use whatever gift you have received to serve others, as faithful stewards of God's grace in its various forms," (1 Peter 4:10-11).

- Peter Johnson

Michael Paddock, known for engineering brilliance and narrative flair, has long been one of America's best exports, leaving behind a legacy of bridges to cross and clean water to drink. His new book, *Global Inspirations*, which illuminates faithful men and women in Africa and Central America, reminds readers at a time of resurgent nationalisms that "God has made of one blood all peoples of the earth" (Acts 17:26).

- David Douglas, principal at Global Water 2020,
and author of *Wilderness Sojourn,*
Pilgrims in the Kingdom,
and *Letters of Faith*

This book reminds us that while opportunity tends to favor the wealthy, wisdom and faith (gifts from God) are found in every nation, but especially where they are most needed for survival. *Global Inspirations* shows us the importance of both the individual and the community. I very much enjoyed Michael's latest book and encourage all to read it!

- Marilyn Thompson, Missions Coordinator
for Peace Lutheran Church

Global Inspirations shows what happens when engineering is not limited to the top three inches of the brain and brings the heart into the discussion.

- Bernard Amadei, Ph.D., NAE., Founder of EWB-USA

Global Inspirations
Stories of Faith from Around the World

By Michael Paddock

www.ten16press.com—Waukesha, WI

AUTHOR'S NOTE:

This story is based upon actual events.
For the sake of privacy, some names have been changed.

Global Inspirations: Stories of Faith from Around the World
Copyrighted © 2021 Michael Paddock
ISBN 9781645382881
First Edition

Global Inspirations: Stories of Faith from Around the World
Written by Michael Paddock

Cover Designer: Faith Smith
Unless otherwise noted, all photographs provided by Michael Paddock

For information, please contact:

www.ten16press.com
Waukesha, WI

The author has made every effort to ensure that the information within this book was accurate at the time of publication. The author does not assume and hereby disclaims any liability to any party for any loss, damage, or disruption caused by errors or omissions, whether such errors or omissions result from accident, negligence, or any other cause.

I dedicate this book to Paul Johnson (Don Pablo) and Father Gregory Schaffer (Father Greg), humble men who helped so many, both physically and spiritually.

Thank you for your mentorship, inspiration, and friendship.

TABLE OF CONTENTS

Introduction..1

Pollo De Cata. Cata teaches me that faith needs to be patient. God will answer our prayers in his own time, but he is always listening...9

The Power of Hope. My mentor Father Greg shows me the power of encouragement and hope, and the importance of instilling hope in those who have lost hope in themselves...................21

Pastors Are Truly a Blessing. I am reminded that pastors and priests are a blessing I had taken them for granted.....................27

He Who Is Almost Saved Is Totally Lost. I learn that we need to help those who are "almost saved" so that they might truly believe..33

Faith Never Gives Up. The community's midwives inspire me to never lose faith even after years of setbacks.....................38

Bolivian Shoes. I am shown how often I have doubted, or ignored, the power of God and how through him, all things are possible....46

God's Guidance in Afar Ethiopia. I was reminded that God sometimes uses us as instruments to provide his will and we need to be willing participants..53

A Christmas in Bench Maji. I share my experience in celebrating the birth of our Savior in a different, yet interesting culture, and think about how many mothers around the globe suffer in health care facilities that lack basic services..59

The Ghanaians Inspire My Faith. I learn that Sundays are a special gift and should not be taken for granted........................66

Lifting a Heart with a Friendly Smile. I am uplifted by a smile and greeting from a complete stranger who inspires me to share God's love with others..71

A Life Well-Lived. A grandmother inspires me through her lifelong commitment to service of others....................................76

Dominican Faith Shines Through. The Dominicans remind me to give thanks for what we have, even in a time of need.................83

200 Mph Winds Were Not Enough to Shake Their Faith. A Bahamian couple provide me with encouragement after taking the worst that Hurricane Dorian could deliver............................90

Our Homes Were Simply Swept Away. A business owner lets his "Little Light Shine," inspiring his whole neighborhood after devastating Hurricane Dorian..96

Living on a Roof for Ten Days. A woman teaches me the lesson that the building is not important. It is the people who fill it that really matter...103

Judgment. A Filipino grandmother teaches me not to pass judgement on others...110

Healing Together. I am reminded that sometimes we need a friend or neighbor to show us the positive things in our lives after our own personal disaster...118

A Christmas Present at Socorro. A women leader inspires me in this story with her faith in God and by simply saying "Here I am God, send me."...126

Having Faith Can Be Hard. I am inspired by the unwavering attitude and faith of a friend who has so little............................133

Struggling at Home. A Guatemalan seamstress shows me that God's love is even more powerful than COVID-19. He will take the worry and stress from us if we only allow him to...............141

Acknowledgements...151

About the Author...153

Introduction

I have found God's faithful in some of the most unexpected and challenging settings around the globe. It is in traumatic times that we find, and are inspired by, those with faith around us.

As one of my mentors, Paul Johnson told me. "God's love shines through his people in some of the most amazing circumstances. You just need to accept that you are part of God's plan and be willing to open your heart to the inspiration of others."

This book is comprised of short stories that capture my experiences with some of God's most amazing people from around the globe. The stories were originally published in Peace Lutheran Church's newsletter, located in New Berlin, Wisconsin and are reprinted with their permission. The faithful of Peace Lutheran Church have anchored and encouraged my faith for more than three decades. Despite being absent from services for months at a time, I have always felt the encouragement and prayers of the family at Peace.

So how did this civil engineer from Southeast Wisconsin get on an amazing global journey?

My life changed in 1997 when I was thirty-two years old. It was just before Christmas and I went to the hospital for what I thought was an appendicitis attack. I woke up from surgery only to find that I had cancer (non-Hodgkin's lymphoma) and was given less than six months to live. I went through the typical emotions of those with a life-threatening cancer diagnosis—denial, anger, self-pity and finally—acceptance. I had found peace and was ready to meet my maker.

God had other plans.

After five years, I found myself unexpectedly still on this planet and in full remission. What would I do with this gift? I knew that returning to my old life was not an option.

My wife Cathy and I plotted our future to use the gift of life to help others around the world using my engineering skills. That's how this civil engineer who managed multi-billion-dollar projects in Wisconsin became a full-time service engineer, traveling to some of the most impoverished and devastated places on five continents.

Reaching for the stars is only possible when you can stand on the shoulders of giants. Fortunately, God has provided me two amazing people of faith as mentors to guide me in my journey.

The first was Paul Johnson who I met more than twenty years ago. Paul is a civil engineer who has a heart full of compassion and a faith as solid as bedrock. I met Paul while I was working with students from my alma matter, Michigan Technological University, in Bolivia. The student team had just completed a project and needed to return the survey equipment which I had borrowed from a local missionary. (Spoiler alert! You'll learn more about the project in the chapter, 'Bolivian shoes'.)

I was a bit nervous meeting Paul at the Bolivian ice cream store because I was nearly a week late in returning the survey transit. I knew how upset I would be if I had traveled to Bolivia only to find out that the tools used to lay out my project were not available. To my relief, he welcomed me with open arms and an ice cream cone. As we settled into chairs and licked vanilla ice cream, soon we were discussing engineering projects and their details—a habit of most of us engineers. He shared with me his faith and how he had come to serve God around the globe with his engineering skills. Through these discussions, I was hooked.

My mentor Paul Johnson and his wife, Shirley Johnson in Guatemala

Later Paul remembered the story: "You may have gotten the survey equipment for an extra week in Bolivia, but I got you to work on engineering service projects for over twenty years. I think I got the better end of that deal."

Paul connected me to several groups working in Guatemala. It was during one of these early service engineering trips that I first met my other mentor, Father Greg. I was working on a drinking water project that would benefit the pueblo and several communities served by the mission. Father Greg's half century of work at the mission in San Lucas Toliman is legendary and I was excited to meet him.

When I first saw him, I was surprised. He was dressed in an old flannel shirt and looked like he'd just walked off a farm in New Ulm, Minnesota. Could this be the legendary man I'd read so much about? He was casually chatting with those around him about the day's activities. The love and respect between him and the villagers were immediately apparent, and he walked among them as an equal.

Father Greg and I immediately connected over two common loves: the Minnesota Twins and walleye fishing. Both from Minnesota, we'd sit in his office and talk baseball and fishing well into the night. As we shared yarns, Father Greg assured me that the good Lord might overlook a fishing story that stretches the truth.

"After all, Jesus was a fisherman, so he understands," he said with a smile.

Father Greg taught me the meaning of hope—maybe the most powerful emotion God has given to humans. I remember sitting in the dining hall enjoying a cup of the mission's Café Juan Ana coffee—without question the most amazing coffee

I had ever tasted. He told me the stories of how many in the surrounding community would be born, live, work, and die in the same small shack without any hope of a better life. He explained to me the importance and value of giving hope to those who are hopeless. This was a new concept for me because I had never truly been without hope in my life. You will hear more about Father Greg in the Chapter, 'The Power of Hope'.

Father Greg questioning one of my fishing stories

"There may be no better gift to those in need than the feeling of hope: hope in their future both in this world and the next," Father Greg told me.

Through my travel experiences, I have been blessed to find many inspiring Christians who have never lost their faith in God or their hope. I pray that these short stories inspire your hope for this world and your faith, as they have my own.

GUATEMALA

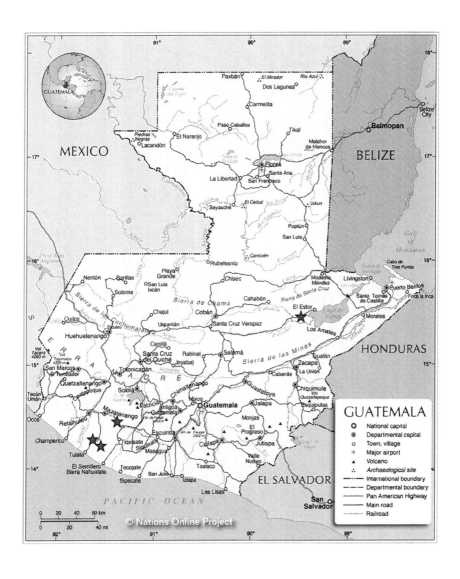

Chapter One—Pollo De Cata

Guatemala Highlands

One of the most inspirational people I've met in my journeys is Catarina, or Cata for short. She's taught me that faith needs to be patient. God will answer our prayers in his own time, but he's always listening. I met Cata in 2013, and she told me her life story.

Cata was born in the rural Guatemala Highlands in the heart of the coffee region. Both of her parents are Quiche Mayan and live a simple life picking coffee beans and doing other odd jobs.

As a toddler, before she could even remember, she suffered a terrible accident. While playing outside of her home, she fell off a high cliff. Her mother was terrified and initially thought her daughter was dead as she stared into the ravine at Cata's small, lifeless body. But she noticed some movement and realized that Cata had survived the fall. She raced down the ravine to her crying daughter, giving thanks to God that her Cata was still alive. Her joy was soon replaced with horror as she realized the extent of her daughter's injuries.

Cata's face took the brunt of the fall and several bones were broken, causing one side of her face to look disfigured.

Thankfully, Cata healed and was soon running around the yard like any other young girl not even knowing that she had suffered such a traumatic event or had a disfigurement.

Her mother protected her and kept her close to home until the time came for her to attend school when she was six years old. On the first day of class, Cata proudly walked to the school. It was a milestone for her because she loved to learn. She had so looked forward to going to school with the older children and becoming a 'big girl'. Soon, the joy vanished.

Almost immediately, the other students made fun of her and her appearance. Cata was confused as they called her a 'monster' and other terrible names. She failed to understand why her new classmates were making fun of her and being so mean, until one of them challenged her to look at her reflection. She found a puddle near the school and in its reflection, saw her face for the first time.

She was horrified. Her face looked like nothing she had ever seen before in the likeness of her family. She gently traced the lines of her face with her hand and realized that she was not like the other children. Quickly, she hid her face and ran non-stop back to her home. There, her mother wiped away the tears and told Cata she did not need to go back to the school and the teasing students. She could help her mother around the home, and she would be protected from the cruel world. Cata lived her life in isolation with her family, always avoiding a mirror or a puddle that might remind her of her appearance.

One day, when she was eighteen years old, Steve, a missionary with Otter Creek Church in Tennessee, stopped by. Steve and his wife Magda had been serving the people of Guatemala for many years, supporting clinics and frequently leading medical missions to the region near Cata's home. It was during one of these missions that a community member told them about Cata and wondered if the doctors might be able to help her.

Steve talked quietly with Cata's mother about the medical team and asked if they might help. He did not know for sure if the doctors could help Cata and cautioned the family to not get their hopes up yet, but he wanted to try. The first step would require Cata to travel to Guatemala City with Steve's family and to be assessed at a hospital near Steve's home. The trip was unimaginable to young Cata who had never left her village and rarely her own home. She was scared.

But with her mother's urging, Cata bravely accepted the invitation to make the trip. She hid her face as she traveled with Pastor Steve to make the day-long trip to the city. At Steve's home, she continued to hide her face and look at the wall to avoid the eyes of any of the family members. She refused to utter even one word. Finally, after months, Steve and Magda's daughters convinced Cata to leave her shell and engage with the family—no small achievement because Cata still only spoke Quiche Maya at the time.

Cata allowed the doctors to examine her injuries with the hopes that reconstructive surgery might be done in Guatemala. But the injuries were too severe. Some of the bone in her face had died and they lacked the equipment in Guatemala to help her. Cata's heart sank because she had prayed for God to allow her to look like her sister.

"All I wanted was to look like other girls for just five minutes. I wanted to know how it felt to be normal," Cata told me.

Now, it seemed that all hope was lost.

Seeing her disappointment, Steve told her to keep praying and have faith that God would help her. He'd work with the medical team to try to find a doctor in the United States who might be willing to help her.

For years, Cata split her time between her home and Steve's family. She continued to cook for the medical teams led by Steve and prayed that a doctor could be found to help her.

"I realized that I not only needed help to fix my face but also heal my soul," she told me.

Cata never lost hope or faith, always knowing that God was listening to her prayers and would answer them in his own time.

Then one day, Pastor Steve shared the good news that he had found a doctor in Jackson, Mississippi who was willing to help and provide his services for free. Pastor Steve said that it would take many months to get the necessary travel papers ready but promised to not rest until everything was in place.

Cata would have to travel to Mississippi and spend two weeks with the surgeons who would operate on her face. Cata was twenty-four years old now and the trip to this far-away land was something she could not even imagine. Cata's mother encouraged her, knowing this was the opportunity she had longed for her daughter ever since that fateful fall.

Pastor Steve explained that a large airplane, just like the ones she had seen in the sky, would fly them high up into the heavens and over the ocean to the United States. Cata prayed, thanking God for hearing her prayers and asked for the strength she would need to make the journey. She felt God's comfort and reassurance that everything would be ok, so she bravely agreed to make the trip.

The day finally came and Cata traveled with Pastor Steve to the airport in Guatemala City. She would fly with Pastor Steve to Miami who needed to attend a meeting there. But the scariest part of the trip was that Cata would need to make the rest of the journey alone from Miami to Atlanta and then to Jackson. Steve assured her that he had made arrangements with the airlines to assist her in her transfers.

Oh, how she trembled when she had to say goodbye to the rest of the family as she and Paster Steve departed for the airport. Cata was so afraid, but Steve never left her side as they wove their way through the mesmerizing maze at the airport. The airport was so loud and strange compared to her home in the Highlands. But she was also looking forward to the flight. Steve had told her that the plane would go up into heaven and she was sure that she would be able to see Jesus high in the clouds.

Cata settled into her window seat and the stewardess helped buckle her seatbelt. The plane taxied down the runway and she fidgeted nervously with her hands. As the plane lunged to take off, Cata felt terrified. Was this normal? She looked around and saw that the other passengers were not upset, so she hung onto Steve's arm and tried to breathe. Soon the plane left the ground and soared up into the sky. Cata knew that she had to focus on the view out of her window or she might miss her chance to see Jesus.

She was tired from all the excitement but would not allow herself to close her eyes for even a second. She barely allowed herself to blink as she stared out the window waiting for her glimpse of Jesus. She searched and searched the clouds, but Jesus never did appear. As the plane landed with a sudden jolt in Miami, she was so disappointed. How could she have missed her chance to see Jesus? She had never stopped looking out the window. Was Jesus even in this strange new land called the United States?

She followed Steve off the jetway and soon found herself standing in a sea of people in the terminal. Steve smiled at her and told her to take a deep breath as he took her to the gate for the flight to Atlanta. Since she only spoke Quiche, he pinned two letters to her coat, one with an explanation in Spanish and the other in English.

She bravely waved goodbye to Pastor Steve as she walked down the jetway where a smiling stewardess greeted her and Cata handed her the boarding pass. The stewardess realized that Cata was afraid, so she helped her to her window seat and buckled her seatbelt for her. Now she was alone during takeoff and she felt that her heart would pop out of her chest as the plane took off. Once again, she stared out the window looking for Jesus in the clouds. She was determined to not miss him this time. But he never appeared.

In Atlanta, she followed the other passengers off the plane. Steve had made arrangements for someone to help Cata navigate the airport, but somehow the communication had failed, and she found herself alone, standing in the terminal. She had no idea what to do and could not read any of the signs. She then saw a large Black man standing in the terminal. To this day, Cata refers to the man as 'her angel' and she believes that Jesus sent him to help her. She walked bravely up to the man and presented him the letter in English that she had unpinned from her coat.

The man quickly read the letter and smiled at her. He grabbed her by the hand and took her to a restaurant and ordered her a cheeseburger—the first American cheeseburger she had tasted in her life. After lunch he took her by the hand and they walked through the terminal where they got into a limousine to shuttle them to the next terminal. Cata had never seen such a large car before and marveled at the soft seats and smooth ride.

"I think I could have fit my whole village inside that car," she later remarked to me.

After a short drive, they arrived at the correct terminal and 'her angel' took her to the gate for the flight to Jackson.

As the plane rose up into the heavens, she again stared out the window hoping to catch a glimpse of Jesus. But now she knew God was with her. He had sent her an angel to help her and she could feel his presence. She knew she was going to be okay.

She was greeted by the doctor and a translator as she exited the plane, and the doctor took her to his home. He explained to Cata that he would need to put her to sleep at the hospital to perform the surgery but promised to always be by her side. Cata was afraid as they entered the hospital. It was so large and strange.

"I knew it was going to be okay." She told me. "I could feel 'my angel's' presence always by my side."

The surgeon was able to rebuild some of her cheek bone and other facial structure. After her initial recovery, she met Steve again in Miami and then flew with him to Guatemala City. As she continued to recover at Steve's home, she carefully traced the outline of her swollen face with her hands each day when she changed her bandages. Much progress had been made but her face was still disfigured. Steve promised that he would continue to look for someone to help her and asked her not to give up.

One day with Cata now being twenty-six years old, Steve gave her the good news. He had found a doctor who would help and she would come with his family to live in Nashville, Tennessee as the family transitioned back to life in the United States.

For eight years, Cata lived with Steve and his family who lovingly cared for her.

"They are my adopted family," she told me. "I am so lucky to be blessed with two families!"

She underwent many surgeries as the reconstruction process continued on her face. The progress was slow because some of the procedures worked and others did not. But she was not discouraged and even took advantage of the time to learn both Spanish and English from her adopted family members who gladly helped her practice new words.

"Even when I was so tired at the end of the day, I was determined to learn Spanish and English. I felt so lucky to live with such amazing teachers," she told me.

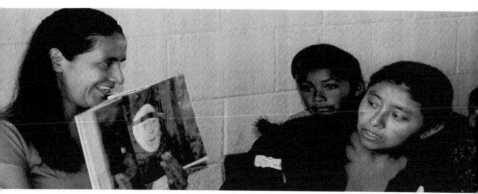

Cata recounting a book to her listeners. Photo Credit: Kevin Colvett

She also learned her numbers and mathematics and grew more confident every day.

During this time, it came to light that Cata had a disability that would prevent her from learning to read and write. But God had given her the gift of an almost perfect memory to compensate. She could repeat a book after hearing it only once. She now speaks fluent Spanish, English, Quiche and several other Maya languages conversationally.

"When God closes one window, he always opens other," Cata always says with a smile.

The day came when no more surgeries would be done. Her face was fully healed, and it was time for her to return home to the Guatemalan Highlands. She loved her Tennessee family so much and knew that she would miss them terribly. But she also longed to see her family in Guatemala whom she had not seen in eight years. She was now thirty-four years old and she had so many stories to share with them about this strange land in Tennessee.

When she finally returned home, the family celebrated her return with a large party. The culture shock was intense as she transitioned back to rural Guatemalan life from her life in Tennessee. She helped her mother with household chores and walked three miles from her house with her father to pick coffee beans, which was the family's main source of income. Oh, how she hated picking beans because she feared the snakes that lurked in the coffee trees, waiting to be startled by an unsuspecting picker.

"I always say a prayer before entering a coffee plantation. I ask God to guide the snakes away from me. I hate snakes," she told me, shaking her head.

She stayed connected to her Tennessee family and the church community there. Several times a year, the church sent a medical mission group to Guatemala to host a clinic in one of the Highland communities. It was during these trips that Cata realized she could help. Her ability to speak Quiche, Spanish and English would make her an important member to any team.

"I knew what God wanted me to do. I would help my people with my translation skills," she told me.

I was introduced to Cata by Kevin Colvett during the construction of a water treatment project in the Highlands. Kevin is a volunteer engineer from Tennessee. He had lived in Guatemala with his family for a year helping the faith-based organization Living Water Project (www.livingwaterwells. org), provide drinking water to rural communities. Cata lived with the family and supported the projects with her translation, but also learned how to support the community development aspect of the projects through communication and capacity building. Cata continues to support Kevin with his work in Guatemala to provide clean water for those who are in need.

After Kevin introduced us, Cata and I soon became fast friends and worked together on many projects from that day forward. We make a good team with me bringing the technical skills and Cata being the community liaison.

"Things always go better with Cata," I like to say.

She is always so positive and never says a negative thing about anything or anybody. Long ago she lost her shy personality and now loves to engage with new people and communities.

"God has not only healed my body, but also my soul," she

Cata with a coffee seedling

told me. "I know he loves me, and I love him. My accident was a blessing as I have met so many amazing people and can now help my people."

Communities are drawn to her and her cheerful disposition. She carefully explains the customs and behaviors of these strange 'gringos' from the United States and quietly dispels any fears or concerns from the community.

Cata loves to cook and her meals are legendary, especially her special chicken, "Pollo de Cata." It is her love of cooking that also endears her to the communities she works in because she easily fits into the community's meal preparation. Cooking is a very important part of the Mayan culture and traditions, and Cata is soon absorbed into the community.

I have come to refer to her as my 'secret weapon'. Time and again, we would visit a community for the first time with the men meeting to discuss the project and Cata finding her way to join the ladies preparing a meal. Inevitably, I would hear a 'holy commotion' erupt from the kitchen as Cata and her newfound friends bonded over the making of tortillas.

On our way home from the visit, we'd have a debriefing. The team would share what we learned from our meetings with the community's men. Then Cata would tell us 'the real story', giving us the background and concerns of the community that she learned from her new cooking friends.

I thank God every day for putting Cata into my life. I don't know where this woman who weighs less than a sack of cement gets her strength and wisdom. Time and again, when I am getting frustrated with a project, she'll come and sit with me. We'll pray together and allow God to accept our worry and provide us comfort.

"You need to be more patient," she always tells me. "God is always listening, and he will respond to our prayers in his own time. You just need to have faith."

Chapter Two—The Power of Hope

San Lucas Toliman, Guatemala

November 2005

The community of Nueva Providencia is located in the heart of Guatemala's coffee plantations near Lake Atitlan. The coffee grows on the side of Volcano Atitlan whose rich volcanic soil and high elevation provide the perfect conditions for some of the world's best coffee. The rich vegetation with views of the volcano in the background provide some of the most amazing landscapes I have ever experienced.

A breathtaking view of Volcanos Atitlan, Toliman and San Pedro

In 2005, many people were displaced due to the threat of landslides after Hurricane Stan. Fortunately, the Catholic Mission in San Lucas Toliman led by Father Greg Shaffer purchased a coffee plantation, giving the local people a place to build a new life. The plantation would be subdivided into family-sized lots large enough for a home and garden. The lots would be provided to the displaced families who would have a subsidized mortgage and zero interest. Father Greg asked that I help lay out the home lots and insisted that each lot was _exactly_ the same size to ensure fairness—a task that would intrigue any land surveyor.

The homes would be located on one side of a lovely river that flowed from volcano Atitlan to the Pacific Ocean. The sound of the flowing water was relaxing, and the stream made a perfect setting for the new community. But the river also created a barrier to the local roadway for the new residents. The roadway was the only connection to the nearby town. Since the river was impassable for six months of the year, the residents requested a bridge to provide the needed access to schools, clinics, and markets.

I was reminded of the words from my Mentor, Paul Johnson. "If you are Pro healthcare, Pro education or Pro economic development—you are Pro Bridge! Without access to the services, they are useless."

The project's implementation would be done through a three-way partnership. The community would provide all the labor and any local materials that could be gathered such as wood, sand and gravel. The local government and engineer volunteers would provide the other materials such as cement and rebar.

This new community is small with only sixty families. At the meeting where responsibilities were discussed, many people became deeply troubled when I indicated that they would need to gather enough stones to fill six dump trucks. On top of that herculean task, they also needed to gather from the river several dump truck loads of sand and gravel that would need to be washed and sieved by hand.

As Father Greg and I discussed the project and laid out the expectations, the people's heads bowed, and they stared at the ground in silence. Clearly something was troubling them. Finally, the chairman for the project cleared his throat and explained that they were afraid the work might be too much for them to accomplish. The piles of stone needed were so large and they were so few. He explained that he was reluctant to discuss his concerns because he was afraid that the project might be canceled if they told us about their worry and doubt.

They were thankful for the help provided, but "We are scared," said the community's chairman, "that our portion of the work might be more than we can do."

Father Greg's calm demeanor and smile apparently provided immediate relief to the concerned group. We explained to them that with many hands all things were possible and suggested that they do the work over several months, scheduling workdays when they could work together as a community.

"Slow and steady like the turtle," Father Greg explained.

The next weekend, the community started its work. Separate crews were organized to work on the different tasks. Everyone did what they could to pitch in. Grandparents worked side by side with their grandchildren as they gathered and washed the sand from the river. The men passed the heavy stones to each other, and carefully stacked them on the riverbank. This was repeated nearly every weekend and slowly, the piles of materials grew, to everyone's delight. Everyone knew that there would be plenty of challenges ahead, but now they knew that if they worked together and encouraged each other, anything was possible.

It took a year for the community to complete the bridge. One week after Easter we celebrated the accomplishment. The people were so thankful for their new bridge and the access it would provide them to services and a future life. Father Greg blessed the bridge and all its workers, sprinkling holy water on the freshly poured concrete. This was a first for me. I certainly had cut many ribbons for new projects, but this was the only time I had been asked to help sprinkle holy water on a project. After many speeches and a few tall tales, the people asked if I could come forward to receive a small gift. They thanked me.

Not for the help—but for the confidence I had in them.

The hand-carved wooden turtle gift to remind me 'Slow and steady like a turtle.

They thanked Father Greg and me for having faith in them, even when they did not have faith in themselves. Then they presented me with a small, hand-carved wooden turtle in honor of Father Greg's words of encouragement, "Slow and steady like the turtle."

This was the first of several projects I worked on with Father Greg and I considered him to be one of my mentors. One of the many things that he taught me is the value of hope. The gift of hope and encouragement is often the most powerful gift we can give each other—especially when we are hopeless. God gives us hope through our prayers. We also support each other in times of despair by giving encouragement and hope.

The simple act of listening to a friend in need can be so helpful in times of hopelessness.

"A problem shared is only half a problem" is an old Mayan saying.

I visit Nueva Providencia at least once a year and look forward to enjoying a cup of some of the best coffee in the world with my friends. The original makeshift homes made of plastic and tar paper have given way to concrete block homes that have water and electricity. An elementary school has been built and even expanded as the community has grown. Children cross the bridge to get to the high school and the Catholic mission's hospital and church is only a short ride away. Hope continues to live on in the people's hearts and even more projects are planned.

Of course, the wooden turtle holds a special place on my desk in Wisconsin. I take encouragement from it in my times of "hopelessness" and think of the gift that my friends at Nueva Providencia gave to me.

Father Greg Schaffer. 1934–2012

Learn more about how his work continues at www.sanlucasmission.org

Chapter Three—Pastors Are Truly a Blessing

El Estor, Guatemala

November 2007

This region of Guatemala is located where the flat jungle plains start to give way to the rising elevation of the Highlands. The area is much warmer given its coastal elevation with lush and varied vegetation as compared to the mountains. The homes are made of grass with thatched roofs and the land yields plenty of fruit and vegetables.

For many years, Father John had visited the community every two months to lead the faithful parishioners in a mass. In between visits, the people continued to lead their own prayer services—but oh how they looked forward to Father John's visits and his inspirational messages! When Father John came, the people celebrated his arrival by going "all out" and hosting a special meal and a full day of worship. What a blessing to be led by a called and ordained leader—a real treat!

But for four months of the year Father John was unable to visit the community because access was blocked by a river. The people were completely isolated during this rainy period and he saw how they suffered without access to schools, clinics and markets. He hoped to help them gain reliable access to these important services and to allow him to reach his flock throughout the year.

Father John is a traveling priest, meaning he's responsible for providing spiritual guidance for dozens of communities in the area. His quiet and humble nature was reflected in his request for the bridge. Through his travels he sees tremendous need in many communities and knows that many more suffer around the world. Having heard from other priests about the bridges we had built in other parts of the country, he asked if we could help. He explained that this was his top priority to help his flock and asked us to prayerfully consider the request.

When I visited the bridge site the first time, I could not help but be impressed with Father John's dedication. The community was a full five-mile walk from the nearest road on a narrow and winding path. As we walked the four-hour trek, we came to several streams that I thought were the bridge site.

"We can wade or swim this river," the people told me. "Ahead is the larger river where we really need a bridge."

So, we took off our boots and pants and waded through the waist deep water and then continued our journey. Finally, exhausted and covered in sweat, I reached the site. I could see that the community had tried to make a suspended bridge out of barbed wire. Of course, barbed wire is not made of the correct metal to create a cable, so the bridge had quickly failed. The people explained they had worked for months on the bridge, only to have it collapse when the first few travelers tried to cross. Fortunately, nobody was hurt, but they felt discouraged. They had done the best they could, but they needed some help.

A pedestrian bridge was technically possible. However,

A young girl begins to wade the river near El Estor

getting the needed materials to the site was the challenge. We could use local trees for the wood, and the river would yield stones, sand and gravel after the people gathered, washed and screened the material—but we would still need to haul hundreds of sacks of cement, that weighed nearly 100 pounds each, to the site. The thought of transporting the cement five-mile on the winding and steep path was daunting.

I asked the community if they might have horses or mules that we could use. This started a long discussion to the side that lasted nearly an hour. Finally, after much hand waiving, they reported back to me that they only had one mule among all the families. I never did understand why it took a full hour to count to one!

Since the community had only one mule, we searched for

a mule pack train we could rent to provide the transportation. Father John worked his network looking for a mule train to deliver the cement, but each prospect quickly faded once he explained the route. No team owner would risk his animals on such a journey with such heavy loads. I began to worry that a solution might not be possible, but Father John was not to be discouraged.

"God will provide a solution. We just need to be patient," he said.

After several months of searching, Father John called to let me know the search was over. The community members could no longer wait, so they had moved the cement on their backs down the trail by themselves! I tried to imagine them carrying the heavy sacks of cement along the trail and wading the streams. My, how they wanted that bridge!

Next came the transportation of the cables. Every cable had to be walked up the path with nearly one hundred workers carrying it. Each cable looked like a centipede as it snaked its way up the path. After the trip was repeated five times, we were ready to build the bridge.

During four-month construction, the community's energy increased each day as they saw their dream being realized. Each morning I rolled out of my tent and tried to shake off the stiffness of the previous day, only to be greeted by a group of workers with broad smiles and happy chatter. I could not help but be swept up in the excitement.

Finally, they celebrated the opening of the bridge. Father John gave a special sermon from the bridge itself while his congregation sat listening intently on the bank of the river. What joy must have been felt that day knowing they now had

A new bridge is born near El Estor

access to markets, schools, health care—and knowing Father John could come and lead worship during the entire year.

It reminded me of what a blessing we have at my church, Peace Lutheran in Southeast Wisconsin. Many times, I reflect about how "spoiled" we are having access to markets, schools and health care without giving it a second thought. But that day I was reminded how spoiled I am having unlimited access to the church and Pastor. The people of El Estor reminded me to give thanks to God for the opportunity to worship with my brethren at Peace under the careful guidance of our Pastor. I will no longer take him for granted.

Chapter Four—He Who Is Almost Saved Is Totally Lost

Guatemala Highlands

January 2018

When I was in Accra, Ghana, I took note of a billboard. It read. "He that is almost saved, is totally lost."

It struck me as an interesting message, especially for a billboard. I pondered its wisdom and the fact that those who almost believe will never enjoy salvation.

It made me reflect on the bridge project that was completed in San Antonio, Guatemala. The story was the same one I had heard so many times before—a bridge was needed for the people to cross the river and get to health care facilities, schools, churches, and markets. The community is located near the Pacific coast, which along with its lower elevation, brings heavy rains that swell the rivers quickly and with little warning. During larger storms, the rivers may be impassable for many days or several weeks.

Ingrid, the community's leader, was committed to help her neighbors in any way she could. She braved the river, crossing it most weeks to obtain medicine needed by those who feared crossing the waters and being swept away. But some weeks she was unable to cross the raging torrent and had to deliver the news to her neighbors that they'd have to stretch their medications until the waters receded. They'd then pray for the wild river to recede and closely watch the water for when Ingrid might safely cross.

Each day, parents had to make the decision if it was safe to send their children to school. Even if the children could wade the river in the morning, there was always the risk that an afternoon thunderstorm might leave them stranded on the other side away from their home. Sometimes children had to spend several days in the school separated from their parents before the river could be crossed again.

This project did have access to resources that many did not. The City of San Antonio is located on one side of the bridge crossing. The city has small taxis called "tuk tuks" that are available to shuttle people, especially the most vulnerable to their destinations for the price of one dime. If they had a bridge, the tuk tuks would be able to cross the river and provide needed transportation to those unable to walk. The elderly and pregnant women were especially looking forward to crossing the bridge in a taxi to reach the clinic instead of trying to brave the river crossing or remain suffering at home.

I was surprised when I visited the site the first time. I could not help but notice that all of the members of the bridge committee were women! The region's *machismo* society would typically have a 'men only' committee, but these ladies were clearly in charge. When I returned a few months later, two of the five ladies were pregnant. As I looked at these expectant mothers, I fully understood the driver of the project and its urgency.

The ladies under Ingrid's leadership were well organized and ran a tight ship. Anyone who did not pull their weight by volunteering their time at the construction site was soon visited by one of the ladies and received a sternly worded pep talk. These organizers were also good negotiators when purchasing materials; most businesses were able to offer 'one more discount' when looking the expectant mothers in the eye.

Under the strong leadership of Ingrid and her committee of women, the project was completed on schedule and budget

I am standing with the bridge committee of San Antonio.
Photo Credit: Fermin Ortega.

and I wondered if I should have them manage my engineering projects in the United States.

During the construction of the bridge, many kept asking me if I was sure that the bridge was strong enough for the weight of the tuk. I explained that the bridge would hold twenty full-grown bulls at the same time, and they all laughed and smiled.

We completed the construction in three months and the ladies jointly cut the ribbon, opening the bridge at the inauguration. The first taxi driver was summoned and approached the bridge slowly. He got out of the tuk and asked me again if the bridge was strong enough to support his vehicle—his prize possession and livelihood. I assured him that it was more than strong enough to support his taxi and many more. But, after rubbing his chin, he shook his head and refused to drive across the bridge.

A tuk tuk making the trip across the bridge

"I trust you, Engineer, but I am still not sure," he said sheepishly.

After some negotiations, I gave him the deposit of my pickup's keys and the taxi owner allowed me to drive his tuk across the bridge by myself. Everyone cheered once I made it safely across. After the first successful crossing, others quickly followed.

Later that morning, one grandmother rode across the bridge with me in the taxi for the first time and she asked me to stop it in the middle of the bridge. She looked over the landscape, remarking how the river now looked different. It was no longer an ugly, dangerous barrier for her. It was now a beautiful gift from God that she could enjoy safely from the new bridge.

The full benefits of the bridge could not be realized until the community truly believed that it would support them and the taxi. They trusted me, but still had some doubt that held them back from realizing the full benefits of the project. It was not until someone showed them the way and drove the first taxi across that they enjoyed the full benefits.

I then realized our job as people of faith. We need to help those who are "almost saved, but totally lost." We must help those who almost believe and whose doubt prevents them from the joy of salvation.

We do this in many ways. Sometimes we encourage each other in our time of doubt; sometimes we pray together; and sometimes we may need to lead the way by example and encourage others to follow us as we walk our path as believers.

Chapter Five—Faith Never Gives Up

Guatemala Highlands

January 2018

This report comes to you from a rural Guatemalan mountain village named Chupoj. The name Chupoj comes from a locally grown tree that has a special meaning to the Mayans. The tree's bark has been used for centuries as paper to capture the writings of the Mayan people. The ancient Mayan civilization was one of the few around the globe that passed down its history and learning from one generation to the next through writing. Sadly, the conquistadors wanted to stop the practice of the Mayan writings, so they cut down all the Chupoj trees they could find. Fortunately, a few trees survived, and they are cherished to this day by the highlands people, and in this case, celebrated in the name of the village.

Four women, descendants of the ancient Mayans had requested assistance from Rotary for a potable water system for their eight hundred and forty members and I had volunteered to help with the engineering. During my first site visit, I met with the community's four midwives who provide healthcare to their community without benefit of the most basic foundation for health: clean water. Midwives are on the front lines of the community's healthcare system, treating everything from a machete cut to malaria.

I'm with Donnas Maria, Delores, Juana with baby, and Tomasa.

During the rainy season, the people in the community could harvest enough drinking water from their roofs. But, during the dry season, water came only from the dirty river at the base of the mountain. People had to walk three hours down a steep mountain path and back up with a forty-pound jerry can of water. Childbirth was an especially worrisome time for the midwives because they needed to make sure they had ample water on hand for the delivery. They'd instruct a family to pray for rain as the mother's delivery date approached. If no rain came, family and neighbors would make twenty trips with five-gallon containers to the river below to obtain the contaminated water.

As I listened to the community's stories, it became clear that nearly every family had suffered the tragic loss of a child due to waterborne diseases. This sad story was shared by all four ladies who asked for help through the Rotary Club.

This girl helps carry water in advance of the birth of her new sibling.

Quiet tears spilled down Donna Tomasa's face as she told me how water had played a different but equally tragic role in the loss of her own baby. Tomasa was pregnant and was helping carry water up the mountain for another woman's childbirth. Tired, she slipped and tumbled down the steep mountainside. She lost her child.

Then Donna Maria allowed her frustrations to spill out. How could they provide quality healthcare without clean water? These health care professionals know that the dirty river water causes infections, especially in babies and new mothers. They'd done their best, but they knew their neighbors would continue to suffer without access to clean water.

The community had previously tried to establish a reliable and safe source of water. They had requested help from the municipality, who after conducting a study, recommended that a well be drilled. Five years before my visit, they had waited patiently as a drill rig filled the valley with noise as it bored six hundred and sixty feet into their mountain. But no water appeared in the well. Three years later a larger drill rig came and pushed a borehole more than one thousand feet, shaking the mountain for weeks. A water tank was even built—surely God would give them water. But, again, no water appeared in the well and the water tank stood empty as a physical reminder of their dashed hopes.

All four ladies shook their heads as they told me the story, remembering that fateful day. They told me of how they stared at the empty water tank and how their hearts sank. Had God abandoned them? Was God punishing them? They felt it might be time to give up and move their homes to another community.

Then they remembered that God had given them life and each other. A community meeting was called to discuss the challenge. At the meeting, they refused to give up and decided to look for other solutions. There must be another way. A group of elders searched the river valley and finally found two remote springs a mile away and more than a thousand feet below the village. Those springs are what brought me to this mountain hamlet in rural Guatemala, sitting across from these four remarkable keepers of the community's health. Their request to me was simple. They wanted me to determine if the springs provided sufficient clean water to meet the community's needs before purchasing the springs and the land around them.

With the assistance of several men from the community, we measured the quantity of water provided by the springs and

Measuring the flow of the spring and taking water samples

tested it for contamination. At a meeting of all the inhabitants I reported the results back to the community that the water was sufficient to meet their needs and it was safe to drink. They stared at each other for a second and then applauded with joy. Then they bowed their heads and said a prayer of thanks to God for the springs.

The community and Rotary next needed to build the pumps and pipes to get the water up the one-thousand-foot-tall mountain to the existing storage tank. The tank would then feed a distribution system to provide safe water to every household. The work was grueling. First, a mile long path was constructed down the side of the mountain through the forest using picks and shovels. This allowed work teams to carry the hundred-pound sacks of cement on their backs down the mountain to build spring boxes to protect the springs from contamination. Then, one by one, the hundreds of galvanized metal pipe could be walked down the path to build the pipeline.

After months of backbreaking work by the community's work teams, water flowed out of the household taps for the first time. Delores let it flow through her fingers as she giggled like a little girl and did a dance. All her life, she had to fetch water for her family. Just like her mother, her grandmother, and her great-grandmother. Now she knew that her daughters and granddaughters would no longer have to do the labor of beasts of burden. She also knew that the health of her community would be transformed from this day forward.

As we celebrated, I looked into the smiling faces of these four ladies and was amazed at how they had refused to lose faith. Over many years of suffering from the lack of clean water and the terrible setbacks of drilling two deep wells that failed to provide water, they refused to lose faith. Would my faith be so strong?

As we said our prayers of thanks and finished our last tortilla, I watched these four healthcare giants, who barely stood five feet tall, walk away down a path lined by corn stalks towering above them. I knew this project was more than a good idea. It meant a better life for generations to come. I thanked God for leading me to these amazing people whose faith would not be shaken. I thanked God that they would inspire me every day.

Children at the Elementary School at Chupoj.

Bolivia

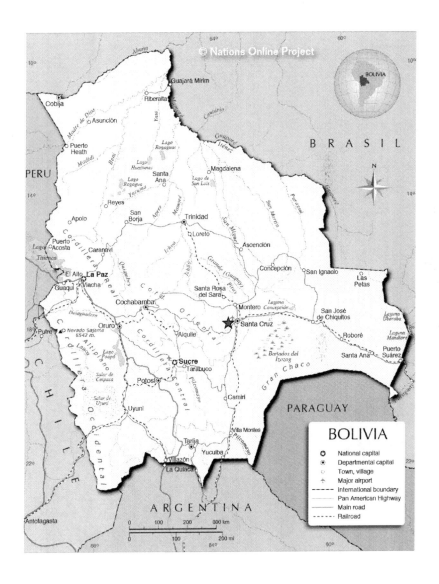

Chapter Six—Bolivian Shoes

Santa Cruz, Bolivia

August 2003

The community of Los Pinos is located on the outskirts of the city, built on marginal land that would generally be considered undevelopable. The homes are built in a random layout and have few services. Life is hard. Most of the members of the community work in the city at various odd jobs, laboring for a few dollars a day.

A few fields growing peanuts were located withing walking distance of the community and the ladies would freshly roast the peanuts dug early in the morning. What a treat to wake up to the smell of freshly roasted peanuts which will soon become the freshest peanut butter in the world. Yum!

A cart delivers milk within Los Pinos.

The community had requested help with a flooding problem that occurred every year during the rainy season. A group of civil engineering students from Michigan Technological University accepted the project as their senior design, or 'capstone' project, and I had agreed to be their mentor.

We learned that the flooding was not so much a wave of water, but stagnant water that stood a foot deep across the entire community for months on end. Since the people used pit latrines for sanitation, you can imagine the putrid, septic state of the stagnant water that saturated their living space.

These conditions were contributing to an unimaginably high infant mortality rate due to early infections. In fact, the women there did not name their children until after the first haircut due to frequent infant deaths. If a woman lost a child before a first haircut, it was considered the same as a miscarriage.

Flooding of putrid water in the community during the rainy season.

Fortunately, after careful study and survey work, a solution was found. Water could be drained to a nearby swamp using a new drainage ditch. The students from Michigan Technological University completed the design, obtaining government approval and consensus with the community. We explained the plan at a large meeting along with our intention to build the project the next year.

Maria, the local leader, interrupted. "God sent me a dream last night and told me that the project would be built now!" she told us with conviction.

We were stunned and politely explained to her that was simply not possible. We needed time to raise funds, organize equipment, and purchase materials. The project would be built, but just not this year.

"I don't think you understand. God is going to build this ditch now and we need to get ready," she said firmly.

As a matter of chance (or maybe not?), we were invited to a school inauguration in a neighboring community the next day. Of course, a group of "gringos" stood out and the Governor came over to talk with us. Maria was there and she seized the opportunity, explaining the situation and asked plainly for his help. How could he say no to such a convincing woman? He promised the use of all the equipment in the area to help with the project.

At this point, I realized the project was going to happen. Now!

The next day, we started to work with the community to construct a drainage canal to move the putrid water away from the homes. The government provided two back hoes, a grader and a dump truck while the people of the community moved

*Drainage ditch construction with the community members
working side by side with the equipment.*

the soil using what they had—wheelbarrows, buckets or dish
pans. The ladies provided food to the equipment operators to
entice them to work well beyond dark, and all were amazed at
the progress.

Finally, after two weeks, we completed the project and a
huge celebration occurred. Maria and her husband, Manuel,
invited us to a simple dinner at their home. The home made
from wood boards consisted of a single room that measured
twenty feet by twenty feet. It was spotless and contained only
a bed, table and a few chairs.

After some chit chat, we sat down and said grace thanking
God for watching over the safety of the workers and the
successful completion of the project. After a simple meal of
rice and beans, Maria and Manuel wanted to give me a gift
to express their appreciation. They handed me a wedding
photo of them taken twenty years previously. I realized it was
the only photo of their wedding that they owned—so I took

a picture of the photo and returned it to them, promising to print a copy for myself to help me remember them.

Manuel would not let me leave empty-handed. He looked around for something to give me and handed to me his next most prized possession—a pair of shoes. I had noticed that Manuel was always barefoot while working on the project, even in the putrid water. He explained that the shoes were only worn on very special occasions such as a wedding or funeral and he wanted me to have them. Of course, the shoes were many sizes too small for me, but he simply refused to take no for an answer.

As I left that night with my new shoes, I could not help but think of the story of the widow in Mark, Chapter 12, who gave the offering of the two mites. How can someone who has so little be willing to give so much? And how can such a small gift have such a significant meaning?

Of course, I never wore the shoes, but still have them and think of Maria's faith often. When God spoke to her, she listened and had faith in his power to help in the face of what appeared to be an impossible task. Her faith never wavered, and she allowed herself to be an instrument in God's plan, despite all of those who doubted—including me.

Yes, it is hard to face the impossible with the faith that God makes all things possible. But then I think of others like Maria who have so much less, yet never doubt the power of God.

I thank God for Maria and her faithful example which inspires me often.

Chapter Seven and Eight locations

Ethiopia

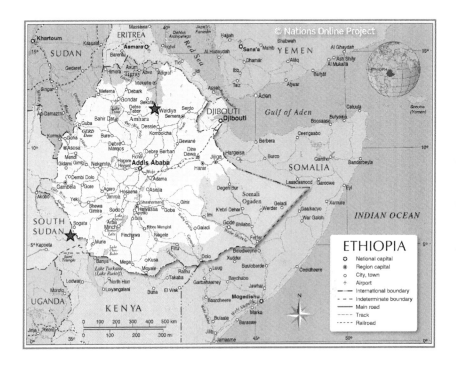

Chapter Seven—God's Guidance in Afar Ethiopia

Zone Three, Afar Ethiopia

June 2016

Eastern Africa was suffering from drought conditions that built up over two years to become an official "disaster designation." You may remember in the 1980's, famines in Ethiopia resulted in more than one million deaths. Determined to not allow such a catastrophe to occur again, the Ethiopian government and world worked to apply lessons from the past to prevent another humanitarian crisis.

I was working with a nonprofit organization as a volunteer engineer as part of the disaster response. The area that we worked in was Zone Four of the Afar Region of Ethiopia in the famous Rift Valley, arguably one of the hottest places on earth. Many believe that early humans originated in this area and the famous "Lucy" archaeological site was only a short distance away. Most of the people in this area are pastoralist, raising goats and camels, moving from one area to the next in search of grass for the livestock.

As I stepped off the plane in Semera, my heart dropped. It appeared that we were too late. Clearly nobody could live in such conditions, I thought. But the Afari people are resilient and were doing their best to hang on. As I looked across the parched earth, it was clear to me that the drought conditions were stressing the herds of animals as well as the people.

I learned that goat herds are the Afari people's bank accounts. Since banks are not available, people store their wealth by buying goats, then sell or trade a goat if they need supplies. Now the goats were dying, and the people were losing everything they had worked so hard for.

Most Afari have two sources of water such as a well or spring. As a backup, the local rivers also provide a source of water when needed. The drought conditions had long ago dried up the surface waters, forcing the communities to rely

A pastoralist's hut in the draught conditions of Afar, Ethiopia.

solely on wells in the area to provide vital water for themselves and their livestock.

In the four-wareda (county) region, fifty wells had been identified that were not working. Access to water was getting desperate. If one of the wells were down, the other well may need to be pumped around the clock to provide needed water. People would wait patiently in line throughout the night with their five-gallon jerry cans for a chance to fill and lug the heavy containers back to their homes.

Things would get more desperate when both wells were down. Typically, this would require the families to make, on average. a six km trek to the next waterpoint in hopes that the community there would be willing to share their precious

A family walks six km to the next water source, hoping that their neighbors might share some water.

water. Everyone was concerned that their water may run out and they might be the next community in desperate need.

The engineering team received a call that the community of Halle Alle was in a dire situation. Their second well had stopped working two days ago and the river was dry. Their neighbors were concerned about sharing water due to a very limited supply. Tensions were high. In fact, some members of the community had traveled the twelve km roundtrip only to return home empty-handed because their neighbors were unable to share their limited water.

When we arrived, I could see the despair on everyone's face. One woman came with an empty jerry can and explained that she had not had any water for two days. She was saving half of a jerry can of water for her children. As she told her story, she started to choke up and looked away. I can only guess that she was imagining what would happen to her family when the water ran out.

Before we started, the local community leader asked for a prayer to grant the engineers the wisdom and strength to fix the well. It was a strange feeling to be asked to be an instrument of God and his work. Many times, we pray that God's will be done and that he uses us as instruments to meet his objectives, but this somehow felt much different and more personal.

I felt God's hand and reassurance as we worked in the 110-degree heat. Somehow, it all felt possible. We sounded the well and found that plenty of water existed in the borehole. As we continued our work, we were excited to find that the submersible pump was in good condition and could easily provide the needed water.

The problem was the large generator set that was broken. It was fifteen years old and replacement parts were no longer available. The day turned into evening as we found a similar part to the one that was broken and forged an adapter so it could be used. We were exhausted but would not stop until water flowed for the anxiously waiting people.

As dusk set in, water started to flow. A huge cry rose from the community and people came running to fill their jerry cans. They cried, cheered and danced all at the same time. With a broad smile, the group elder approached me to express his heartfelt thanks. He said that the community wanted to give me something, but they had nothing—not even a goat.

Then he held out his hand, holding a small shiny rock that he said was very significant for them. He asked that I take the precious stone. I knew declining his offer was not an option. He explained that the stone was a symbol of God's enduring presence and he prayed that God would protect me on my journeys and give me strength to continue to help other people.

This stone now holds a special place in my wallet. I carry it with me wherever I go to remind me that sometimes God uses us as instruments, if we only allow him to do so.

The community's precious stone given to me.

Chapter Eight—A Christmas in Bench Maji

Bench Maji Zone Ethiopia

December 2018

As I bumped along in our Landcruiser, packed in with four colleagues and gear, I could not help but be amazed by the beautiful scenery. We were driving from Addis Ababa, Ethiopia's capital, to the Bench Maji Zone which is part of the Ethiopian Southern Nations, Nationalities and People's Region (SNNPR). The zone is in the far southwest corner of Ethiopia in northeast Africa and we would be working only a few miles from the border with South Sudan. The drive would take a full day—if we were lucky—but I didn't mind as we passed beautiful landscapes and fields that were ripe for harvest.

I watched farmers cut the sorghum grain and transport it by oxen or camel to a central location. There it was trampled by oxen who walked in a never-ending circle while farmers threw the grain under the oxen's feet in order to separate the grain from the stalks. Afterward, the farmers would throw the grain high up into the air to let the wind separate the grain from the chaff. The process had not changed for centuries and the pleasant smell of freshly cut grain filled the air.

Farmers working their field in Ethiopia
the same way they have for centuries.

The Ethiopia Ministry of Health was working hard to improve its rural healthcare facilities. Despite these efforts, many of the facilities still lacked the most basic resource needed for health care—water. Many of the clinics I visited received water only in five-gallon jerry cans carried by donkeys from a river. It is hard to imagine the challenges a lack of water presents to a medical team. Something as simple as washing your hands or cleaning a floor becomes a luxury.

Sadly, Ethiopia is not alone. Even today nearly two billion people on the planet lack access to a healthcare facility that has water and sanitation. As a civil engineer, I find this appalling and have made water and sanitation for healthcare facilities a personal call to action.

Many parts of Ethiopia are Orthodox Christian, which I have found fascinating. The early apostles visited Ethiopia, and the Queen of Sheba came from Ethiopia. Christianity has

Donkeys working hard to carry water for the clinic.
Photo Credit: Haik Kocharian

a long and rich history there. Orthodox Christians believe, like mainline Protestants, in a triune God and Jesus Christ as our Savior. But, since the traditions and customs evolved separately from our own, they have become quite different from those I am used to.

For example, Ethiopian Orthodox Christians celebrate Christmas on January 6th, Epiphany. The celebration is like our own, including a special meal with family and friends as they celebrate the birth of our Savior. Orthodox Christians do not eat meat or any animal byproducts, such as eggs or milk, during Advent. That certainly makes the Christmas feast a time to celebrate as the fast ends and the family dives into their favorite meat and an assortment of cheeses. One would not want to be a chicken or goat on Christmas Eve in Ethiopia!

Since it was a regular workday, on December 25th I found myself helping at a small health clinic, assessing the water supply. The medical team showed me the hand-dug well that no longer produced water. They explained their belief that the well was dry due to the long drought the region had experienced.

As I toured the facility, the medical professionals seemed embarrassed by the lack of cleanliness there. They were doing the best they could without water, but the filth and smell were overwhelming. They knew that healthcare facilities can be transformed from a place of healing to a source of infection simply due to the lack of safe water. They now dared to hope that a solution might be found.

The situation is especially dangerous for expecting mothers. Pregnant women come from the surrounding area, many walking for a day or two, to give birth at the center. One of the initiatives of the Ministry of Health is to provide maternal waiting areas so mothers can travel to the clinic a few weeks prior to giving birth so they can be monitored and receive medical help when the special day comes. This program has saved countless lives.

We entered the maternal waiting area to find a few pregnant women waited in the stick and mud structure that lacked even a sink to wash hands. The clinic's team knows the lack of water is especially dangerous during childbirth and leads to high infection rates for the mothers, their new babies and even the caregivers themselves. There is not a lack of knowledge, but simply a lack of access to water.

Now it was time to assess the existing well. A small crowd had gathered around me as I sounded the well with my homemade tool. My heart jumped with joy as I heard the coveted "pluck" sound when the tool hits a water surface. As the tool continued through the water, I was thrilled to find that more than seven feet of water sat in the bottom of the well—the clinic was home to a virtual swimming pool of clean water! When I shared the news with the doctor, he stared back in disbelief.

"Do you think we could have water soon?" he asked.

"Yes, God willing, I think you will have fresh water by the end of today." I replied. His eyes sparkled. I think he was trying to contain his hope.

We carefully dismantled the pump and pulled the pipe out of the well. We learned that by simply adding another section of pipe, the pump would now extend down into the clean, cool water. We slowly lowered the pipe back down the well, this time a bit deeper and into the groundwater. The people gathered around me anxiously watched as the pump worked for a few seconds before fresh water flowed—and the celebration began.

I have to say it was maybe one of the best Christmas gifts I have ever received in my life when the community clustered around the well holding hands and thanked God for the gift of clean water.

It made me think: Did Mary and Joseph have access to clean water when Jesus was born in the stable?

If you are interested in learning more about how people of all faiths are working to solve the Global Water Crisis, check out http://www.faithsforsafewater.org/what-you-can-do.html. Note this website is not asking for donations, but is simply focused on providing information to churches and people of faith who are interested in the water crisis.

The engineering team and hospital staff celebrate the flow of fresh water for the clinic at the repaired well.

Ghana

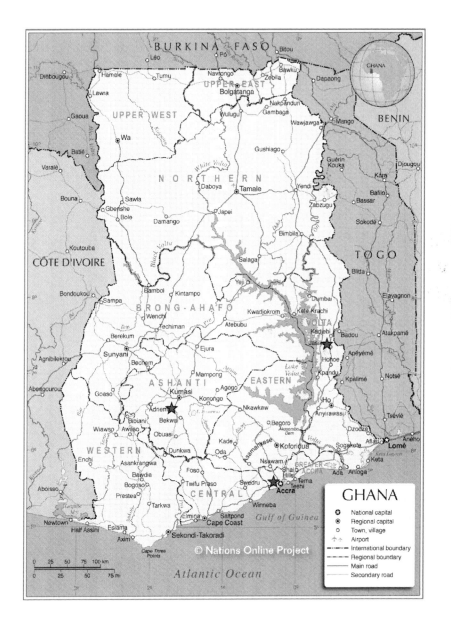

Chapter Nine—The Ghanaians Inspire My Faith

Tongor, Ghana

2016

Ghana is a fascinating country that prides itself on its peaceful existence. It is incredibly diverse with dozens of different tribes that have all learned to work together in this country that is located a stone's throw north of the equator. Each tribe has its own history, culture and structure that must be respected and unlike many other tribal societies', Ghanaians have learned to live and work together in peace. I believe this acceptance of others is why they are so open to visitors from foreign lands. I have always felt welcome in every Ghanaian community I have visited.

A small rural community in Ghana.

I had been working with the nonprofit Safe Water Network, which is helping rural communities "moving up the water service ladder." In many of these communities, people fetch water from contaminated streams or ponds. As in many places around the world, members of the family take five-gallon jerry cans to the fetching station each morning to collect water for the day. Can you imagine carrying forty pounds of water for more than a mile?

Not only is fetching water hard work, but it is very time-consuming to wait in line, fill the jug, and transport the water back home. In fact, one or two girls from each family do this duty and many times don't have enough time to both fetch water and attend school. What an incredible waste as these smart girls are relegated to this duty and not allowed to reach their full potential by attending school.

A girl fetches water for her family.

Things are improving in Ghana. More homes of concrete block are being built and services, such as electricity and household water connections, are now possible. A household connection is something the people previously could only dream about and it can be transformational for a family and even the whole community. You can only imagine the excitement of the women and girls in the community when they realize that they may now have water available at their home.

The people of Ghana are inspiring Christians who strengthen my faith with each and every visit. Christian living is intertwined into their lives and you cannot help seeing it every day. The billboards along the roads are full of advertisements for Christian conventions on the weekends where people gather and strengthen their faith. Businesses typically carry names such as "Jesus is Lord—Bread" and "He is Risen—Mechanics." People's faith is proudly displayed "front and center" in their lives and they are surprised to learn that this is not the case in the United States.

Funerals were maybe the most inspiring to me. They always occur on the weekend and are a large celebration of the person's life. The death announcement is done through posters and flyers with a photo of the deceased and usually a caption such as "Called to Glory." Sometimes a whole billboard will be rented to make the announcement.

The funeral is a whole-day affair, with friends and family celebrating the loved one passing on to heaven. Everyone is well dressed in colors representing the standing of the person in the community. It is a beautiful sight. Yes, there is sadness that the person will be missed on earth, but there is an underlying genuine joy to the event as people know that their loved one is now in heaven. This is not the end, but only a transition to the next phase of one's soul.

Sundays are always reserved for worship and family. Everyone dresses in their Sunday best with many of the women wearing dresses made from the famous *kente* weavings. Church services typically last for several hours, but they don't seem that long to me. The service is filled with singing and dancing and one cannot help but get caught up in the energy. No one reluctantly comes to the service. It seems that everyone truly looks forward to worshiping and it is a highlight to everyone's week. In fact, it was a common topic of discussion during the work week among my friends and coworkers as we worked on the water projects.

On one of my first visits, we were behind schedule on the construction of our water station and I was hoping to make up some time on a Sunday. I made the mistake of suggesting that we might collect some data on a Sunday afternoon for a few hours after church service.

My coworkers stared back at me in disbelief. They seemed to be trying to be careful not to offend me as their guest, but politely stated that they were spending time with their family after worship and work simply was not an option for them. The sabbath is an important day for their faith and family and would not be compromised for any reason. They recognize the importance of taking one day a week to worship, celebrate and enjoy the company of loved ones.

The work at the water station waited until Monday when we worked late into the night to get the project back on schedule. Yes, providing clean water to the community is important but it's also important to enjoy Sundays as a day of worship with friends and family.

I've been inspired by my Ghanaian brothers in Christ and look forward to worshiping with them. Back home, I now look at Sundays in a whole new light. I had slid into a habit of looking at Sunday services as an obligation instead of a special gift. I consider my Sunday afternoons the same as any other day of the week.

Now, with the help of my Ghanaian friends, I have come to appreciate Sundays as the special gift from God that it is.

Chapter Ten—Lifting a Heart
with a Friendly Smile

Accra, Ghana

2017

I had just returned to the city of Accra in Ghana after a grueling week in the field. We were working with the Ghana Ministry of Health and a Ghanaian nonprofit to provide water and sanitation to healthcare facilities. Sadly, most of the rural clinics in Ghana do not have water or sufficient sanitation. Ghana is not alone. It is hard to believe, but two billion people on the planet do not have access to a healthcare facility with water and sanitation, forcing seventeen million mothers to give birth each year in unimaginable conditions. Fortunately, Ghana is one of the leaders in West Africa in addressing the situation and improving the conditions for its citizens.

Even though we had been able to make good progress at several sites, spending so much time in the health centers had taken a toll on me. Watching doctors and nurses try to provide healthcare in a setting where they did not even have water to wash their hands was heartbreaking. But it was seeing new mothers struggling to clean themselves and their infants, all to prevent infections in an environment without safe water, that really captured my soul. I felt frustrated, dejected, and depressed.

As I walked down the street, I was completely distracted thinking about water flow rates, pump curves and pipe loss equations—when a well-dressed woman walked by in a traditional Ghana gown made from the local *kente* cloth. I wore a dirty t-shirt with the words "Water is Life" printed on it. She smiled at me. She pointed at the shirt and said, "Water is Life—Yes!" with a big smile across her face.

I stopped and we started to chat.

Ghanaian weavers making kente cloth.

Her name is Grace, and she was clearly nervous as we started to talk. But after a little chit chat, she told me her story. She had been down on her luck and wondering how she was going to feed her new baby after the father had abandoned them. She was getting desperate and decided to try to raise money by selling small bottles of water to drivers stuck in traffic.

She started at one of the city's busiest intersections, walking up and down the lines of traffic for eight hours a day, trying to sell the water bottles. There were several other ladies selling water and snacks, so the drivers had choices. No matter how hard she tried, she could not get anyone to buy her water. She told me she was getting desperate and feared what the future might hold for her and her daughter.

She then had an idea and started pitching with a tag line of "Water is Life—Buy Some."

"It was amazing. People smiled back at me and began buying my water," she said. "That allowed me to get back on my feet and soon, I was able to find a good job. Now, with God's grace, I am living comfortably with my daughter. So, you see, the phrase "Water is Life" has a very special meaning to me and my family."

It was Sunday and nearly everyone in Ghana goes to church on Sunday mornings, so she asked, "Can I ask if you go to church?"

"Yes, but my church is a long way away. All the way across the ocean in the United States," I responded.

"Are you a Christian?" she asked

I showed her the cross that I always wear around my neck, and she nodded approvingly.

"Why don't you come and join us at our church? It is a wonderful service, and we can grab a bite to eat afterwards."

I looked pretty rough after a week in the field without so much as a shower or shave. I can only imagine how I smelled. She was offering to give me some charity—not the other way around.

I met her and her daughter at the church entrance. We walked into the church together and it was packed with hundreds of worshipers. The building had a large open space with a high ceiling. The chairs were several rows deep and arranged in a semi-circle around the alter. Large windows allowed the sun to wash over us and the open doors and windows allowed the music to spill out onto the street.

I felt so welcome as everyone around us greeted me with a smile and a handshake. It reminded me of my church at home where everyone catches up with their 'regular pew neighbors', exchanging news and greetings in a noisy "holy commotion."

The church service was an amazing three-hour experience of singing, dancing, testimonials, and scripture. It was exactly what I needed to put my thoughts in perspective and energize me for the next week of work. I could feel my soul being restored and energized.

The time seemed to fly by and none of us wanted it to end. We waived goodbye to our fellow worshipers, and I followed Grace and her daughter to a street vendor. We had fufu, a traditional Ghanaian food made from casava roots which is dipped into a spicy soup using one's fingers. We talked about the service, laughed about each other's strange customs, and simply enjoyed each other's company.

I thanked her for her hospitality and as we parted I promised to do my best to return next Sunday—this time after a shower, shave and a change of clothes.

As I walked home, I thought about Grace and her courage. She told me she was nervous talking to me at first. I was the only white person on the street and a man to boot.

"I could see that you were troubled. I knew God wanted me to speak to you and that you needed my help," she said.

I am so glad that her faith was stronger than her fear and provided her courage. How many times have I walked by people on the street in Milwaukee, choosing to look the other way and not even having the courage to say a simple "hello"—let alone engage in a conversation.

She knew that my soul needed to be lifted and offered her friendship at exactly the right time.

I have been inspired by her and now smile and greet strangers as we pass. It is surprising that such a simple gesture breaks down so many barriers and can lead to some lovely conversations.

God wants us to encourage and support each other—be it friend or stranger. I am so thankful that the Holy Spirit sent Grace to me that day. I hope I can pay her support forward to others who might need a little encouragement.

Chapter Eleven—A Life Well-Lived

Kumasi, Ghana

2018

Safe Water Network is a nonprofit organization that designs and builds water systems that pump raw water from a well to a station. There the water is treated and chlorinated under the watchful eye of an operator before it is sent to tap stands where the people can collect it. After construction, Safe Water Network operates the facility without subsidy to ensure long-term sustainability. The water utility's operation and maintenance are supported solely by customers through a fee of less than one penny per gallon of water.

Many nonprofit organizations help provide water to those who lack it, but only a few continue to support the community through the water utilities operation. Cutting the ribbon on a new system is fun and makes great photos, but the real work comes with collecting the tariffs, operating, and maintaining the system. That is why nearly fifty percent of the water systems installed in Africa fail in the first five years through a process I have called "The WASH death spiral."

The WASH death spiral begins when some users refuse or are unable to pay the maintenance fee. The lack of maintenance results in lower-quality water and intermittent service, with water being unavailable for days. More users then refuse to pay the fee due to the poor service. Eventually the system falls into total disrepair. Organizations like Safe Water Network support the operations of the community's water system after its installation, ensuring a sustainable water system for decades.

Hannah is a ninety-three-year-old grandmother and lives in rural Ghana. I met her during a project a few years ago that upgraded her community's drinking water system while I volunteered with Safe Water Network.

Hannah is a 'tap stand vendor,' that is the person who collects three pennies for every five-gallon jerry can of water that is filled at her station. Her job not only includes collecting the fee, but also keeping the tap stand site neat and clean. She washes and disinfects the site twice a day and takes great pride in her work. For every jerry can filled at her station, she receives one of the three pennies for her work. On a typical day, she may fill 300 jerry cans and receive $3 for her daily efforts.

Hannah
Photo Credit: Judy Haselhoef

Hannah prides herself on her job and its impact. Two years ago, her community did not have access to safe drinking water. They fetched contaminated water from a local stream. She told me how she had made the trip to the stream several times a day her entire life, only to wind up with contaminated water. This was the same chore her mother and grandmother made their entire lives. She was fully aware of the dangers of the contaminated water to her community's health and thankful for the improvement.

She explained that the job was perfect for her at her age. She is no longer able to do physical work and her grown children have left the area.

"I stay connected to the news of the neighborhood when everyone comes to my tap for water. My job is important. It gives me money to support myself and gives my life purpose. I love what I do." She beamed.

As I watched her work, it was clear that she was 'the community's Grandmother' as she chatted with everyone, collecting the news and rendering advice for everything from cooking to relationships. She also reminded her customers how to clean their containers and how to keep the clean water safe in their homes. Nearly all the conversations ended with a laugh and a hug. It seemed everyone left happier than when they arrived.

A woman fetching water from Hannah's tap stand.

Four months later, I found myself back in Ghana and needed to follow up on some improvements to Hannah's community water treatment system. But the site was at least a three-hour drive away. It was a Saturday, and I was not looking forward to the day spent in traffic—a common problem for those who travel around the capital of Accra.

But as I bumped along on the dusty road that led to Hannah's community, I soon looked forward to seeing my old friend again. Finally, I arrived and made my way to her home. But something was not right—everything was quiet and strange. When I went to the door, I was greeted by a middle-aged woman who looked tired and distracted. After introducing myself to her, she said that she was Hannah's daughter, and that Hannah was very ill.

I waited at the door while she went back to the bedroom and I heard Hannah say, "My engineer is here! Please send him to me!"

When I entered her room, she struggled to sit up. I helped prop up a pillow under her back under the watchful and concerned eye of her daughter. She was excited to share the news that the water connection was now completed to the health clinic where she has volunteered for years. The clinic workers no longer needed to fetch water from her station because they had their own tap and storage tank.

"The patients and staff can now easily wash their hands at the sink, and it is much easier to keep the facility clean and free from infections," she explained to me.

By now, she seemed very tired, and her daughter made a gesture that told me it was time to leave. I said my goodbyes and gave Hannah's frail body a gentle hug. I swear I could have wrapped my arms around her twice—she was so small. Still, I felt her energy seep into me.

She asked if I would pray with her before I left. We thanked God for the gift of clean water. She asked him to watch over her community, family, and me during my travels. She finished by telling God that she was ready to go home to him and looked forward to seeing her husband who had passed away many years ago.

As I drove home, I felt so glad that I had stopped to visit her. Just like the visitors to her tap stand, I left feeling better than when I had arrived.

A week later, it was time for me to go home. As I waited to board my plane, I got a What's App message from Hannah's daughter. Hannah had been called home, quietly passing away in her sleep.

A life so well-lived.

Dominica

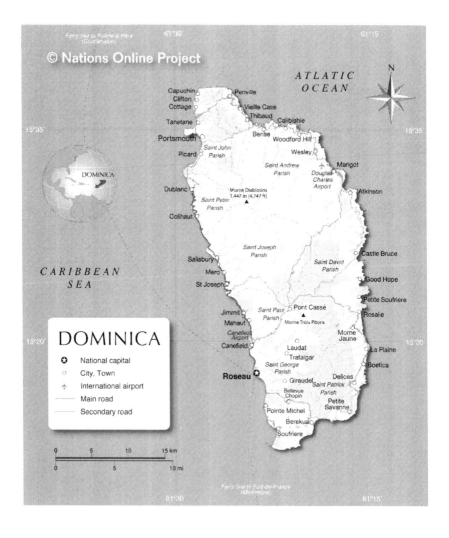

ATLANTIC OCEAN

N

Ferry line to Pointe-à-Pitre (Guadeloupe)

61°30'   61°15'

15°35'   15°35'

Capuchin
Clifton
Cottage
Tanetane
Portsmouth
Picard
Penville
Vieille Case
Thibaud
Calibishie
Bense
Woodford Hill
Wesley

Saint John Parish

Saint Andrew Parish

Marigot
Douglas-Charles Airport

DOMINICA

Dublanc
Saint Peter Parish
Morne Diablotins
1,447 m (4,747 ft)
Atkinson

Colihaut

Saint Joseph Parish

Castle Bruce

Salisbury
Mero
St Joseph
Saint David Parish
Good Hope
Petite Soufriere

CARIBBEAN SEA

Jimmit
Mahaut
Saint Paul Parish
Pont Cassé
Morne Trois Pitons
Rosalie
Morne Jaune

Canefield Airport
Canefield
Laudat
Trafalgar
Saint George Parish
La Plaine
Boetica

15°20'   15°20'

Roseau
Giraudel
Bellevue Chopin
Delices
Saint Patrick Parish
Petite Savanne
Pointe Michel
Berekua
Soufriere

DOMINICA

- ✪ National capital
- ○ City, Town
- ✈ International airport
- ----- Main road
- ········· Secondary road

0   5   10   15 km
0   5   10 mi

Ferry line to Fort-de-France (Martinique)

61°30'   61°15'

Chapter Twelve—Dominican Faith Shines Through

Roseau, Dominica

September 2017

Hurricane Maria hit Dominica with a catastrophic effect. It was one of the most rapidly intensifying storms in history. Roughly twenty-four hours after being upgraded from a tropical storm, it grew to a category five hurricane with some of the strongest winds ever recorded. The storm caught the Dominicans unprepared when it changed its path at the last minute, smashing into their country with a direct hit. The storm battered the country from end to end for nine hours with the eye of the storm traveling the entire length of the island—no place was spared. Literally every home on the island sustained significant damage.

Dominica distinguishes itself from the other Caribbean Nations by its natural beauty and amazing forests. The rugged volcanic topography and national forests have given the country the nickname "The Garden Island." Over the years, many tourists came to walk the nature trails that reached from one tip of the island to the other. After the hurricane, the trees lay on the ground like matchsticks. In some places, the winds blew so hard that they blew the grass from the soil!

*The devastation in the wake of Hurricane Maria
destroying the natural beauty of the "Garden Island."*

I traveled there days after the storm as a volunteer at the
request of the United Nations. The early days were rough—
no shelter, water, electricity, or food. Within twenty-four
hours, the security forces from several Caribbean nations were
deployed to assist the national police in maintaining order.
There were no buildings undamaged to use so they stayed in
the cricket stadium (cricket is the national sport). After I spoke
briefly with the Jamaican Army major, she agreed to allow me
to stay with them.

Our little "stadium community" had to be self-sufficient. We needed to have our own food and clean our own water while living in tents in the stadium. As I opened yet another tin of tuna for supper, my military companions from Martinique offered their meals-ready-to-eat or MREs. I can attest that the French meals were delicious with their sauces and seasoning. The British MRE's?—not so much.

The storm damaged all the island's water systems and the rivers were contaminated with garbage, dead animals and debris. Water supply to the country's citizens was clearly the priority. On my first day three. I started walking from the stadium to the disaster communications center a half mile away. Debris was everywhere. Within the first block, a young mother came up to me in a panic looking for help.

"Sir, can you spare me some water? My child has had no clean water for two days!" she asked with panic in her voice as she pointed to my water bottle.

Of course, I gave her the water bottle, only to see several other mothers now coming to ask for water for their thirsty children. I opened my backpack and soon ran out of water bottles.

Thank God, temporary water treatment plants were established by the government and Samaritan's Purse the next day. The clean water was trucked from the plants to distribution sites around the island to reach for the thirsty people.

A temporary water treatment plant to provide water to a thirsty island. The large settling tanks in the foreground feed the flat storage bladders in the background. People who had cars volunteered to deliver water to community water distribution sites.

The country lived without electricity for nine months. Every automobile on the island was damaged, resulting in most people using their own two feet for transportation. Cellphone service was also down for months, so most residents relied on battery-powered radios to receive the latest news. I smiled thinking how my friends and family back home would go crazy without their phones for even a few hours, let alone months on end.

Dominica is a deeply Christian land. I was told that even before the storm, every government meeting started with a prayer and it ended with a request for God to grant the attendees wisdom and strength to implement his will. This tradition continued during the aftermath of the storm, and I found strength in each prayer. The prayers along with God's presence kept us going despite challenges.

This was the second major storm in two years to hit the Dominican people, and many questioned if God had abandoned them. How could they even think of rebuilding, when they had not repaired the damage from the last storm? Many simply wandered their neighborhood with emotionless expressions on their faces. It seemed they didn't know where to even begin. They were stunned and in shock, barely able to utter a grunt when I greeted them on the street.

But soon, the mood changed. People started greeting each other with a response of "God gives me life," when asked "How are you?" They started the cleanup effort by sorting valuables and sentimental objects from the piles of debris that used to be their homes. Even people's appearance changed; heads of hair were now combed, and beards shaved.

The following week, church services began to be held. Yes, the buildings were destroyed, but that would not stop the people from worshiping their Lord and Savior. People began to focus on what they <u>did have</u> and not what they did not have.

A few months later, it was a difficult Christmas in Dominica. I watched as unexpected rains pelted the island during what is typically their dry season. Spending Christmas under a leaky tarp in a shelter is not what people had hoped for—and I was afraid that their spirit was about to be broken. How much more could they take?

Then, I noticed a transformation. People started to gather at night in neighborhood groups. A few makeshift benches began to spring up and folks sat around their solar lanterns telling storm stories, listening to the radio, and supporting each other. Soon they started to sing Christmas carols. I heard laughter for the first time.

As the lanterns gave out and darkness settled in, the groups always prayed together before going back to their dark shelters. The prayers were not asking for help, but for thanksgiving. Thanksgiving for their faith, family, and friends.

I know many challenges lie ahead for these faithful people, but I cannot help but be inspired by their faith. I know that with God, all things are possible, and I thank my Dominican friends for inspiring me in my faith. I think of them every day.

A homeowner showing his Dominican spirit.

The Bahamas

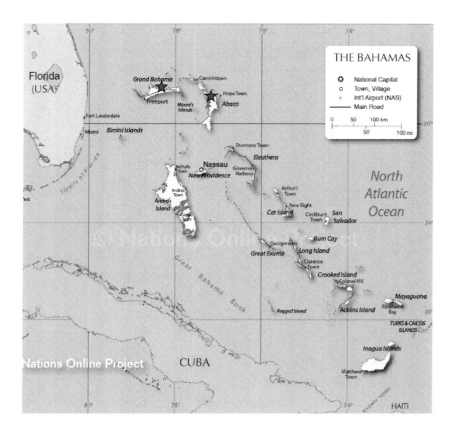

Chapter Thirteen—
200 Mph Winds Were Not Enough
to Shake Their Faith

Abaco, The Bahamas

September 2019

"Mike, I don't know where you are, but can you come to the Bahamas? It's pretty bad."

It was my colleague from the United Nations just hours after Hurricane Dorian had made landfall. The category five storm had stopped over the islands and hammered them for an unprecedented two days with intense rains and winds over 200 mph that refused to relent. I had seen the terrible images on TV and expected a call.

"When do you need me?" I asked.

"Tomorrow would be fine."

The next day I found myself on a humanitarian flight to the Bahamas as part of the engineering team assisting with the Hurricane Dorian disaster. We arrived in Nassau, the nation's capital that had been spared by the storm. Fortunately, the capital was intact, and the city was abuzz with energy from relief organizations. The Bahamas is no stranger to these devastating storms, with a hurricane making landfall on average every four years. But this was the most intense storm to hit in the 170 years of recorded Bahamian history and nobody could have been prepared for its impact.

The day after our arrival, we were on Abaco Island, which had been the first island to be hit by Dorian. Fortunately, the government had provided a warning to the island's residents days in advance of the storm making landfall, and some of them had evacuated using the ferry to Nassau. But many of the island's most vulnerable residents, who lived in the informal settlements of "The Pea" and "The Mudd," had no place to go to and were forced to shelter in place during the incredible hurricane.

Portions of Abaco Island were completely destroyed by Hurricane Dorian.

After the storm, the government made the difficult decision to fully evacuate the island due to the devastation and the complete lack of services. The first responders worked hard to evacuate the survivors and the ferry pier had been put back in service. People looked stunned as they walked silently to the boat with what few possessions they could carry.

In some areas the destruction was nearly total. There was incredible damage everywhere I looked. Once we left the ferry site, the island was like a ghost town. The only way to navigate through the rubble was by foot. The debris made it difficult to even see where the roads had been, let alone drive them. Water systems, electricity and cell phone service had been totally wiped out. The emptiness gave me an eerie feeling, and the stench of rotting waste was at times overwhelming. We worked our way from community to community and the days started to blur together as we assessed the damage and started to develop a response plan.

Mentally, I was wearing down and feeling a bit overcome. The impact was so extensive, and the need was so widespread. Where could we even start? It was becoming clear that it was going to take years to rebuild.

Then I saw some movement in the distance at a home that had been partially blown away. I was afraid at first, thinking it was another pack of stray dogs roaming the island. As I cautiously approached, I could see it was two people who were not part of the engineering team. Strangely, they looked happy.

An old couple were sitting on the steps and greeted me with a smile and a wave. Wilma and Martin introduced themselves and calmly invited me to have a seat on their stoop. They had lived in the home most of their lives and raised their family there. Thankfully, they were uninjured, and peppered me with questions, seeking information about the impact on their friends and neighbors. I asked if I could help them to the evacuation point, but they declined.

This school bus was no match for Hurricane Dorian's winds.

"This is not our first hurricane, you know—but it was a doozy. We stocked up on canned goods before the storm when we heard the warnings and we have a water cistern that catches the rainwater, so we are well supplied. We're just fine—but thanks for asking," they said. I saw determination in their eyes.

After inspecting the home, I determined that there was a portion that was safe for them to occupy but asked if they might reconsider evacuating since they would be all alone and without electricity and running water for some time.

"We are islanders," Wilma explained. "We know how to make do. Martin may not look like much, but he is stronger than he looks. We will be fine." Martin beamed at his wife's compliment and puffed out his chest.

They told me the story of how they took shelter in one room, only to be chased to another portion of the house as windows broke, roofs were destroyed, and water rose. Their home had a second story, so they ended up riding out the worst of the storm upstairs in a closet. As we passed through the living rooms, I saw a crucifix on a shelf.

Wilma noticed, saying "He watched over us during the worst and he will keep us safe now." She asked if I might pray with them, and of course I said yes.

Wilma thanked God for keeping them safe and for their daily bread. She then asked him to bless me and keep me safe. She asked God to strengthen my heart. I think she could see the weight the devastation was having on me. She asked nothing for her, her family or home.

I asked her, "Didn't you ever doubt your faith during those awful two days?"

"I'm ready to go when the good Lord takes me. I hung onto Martin and he hung onto me. We figured if we were going to go, we might as well go together," she said with a smile.

As I left, I gave them my granola bars, two flashlights, and all the spare batteries I had. Wilma gave me her son's phone number and asked that I get word to him as soon as I could that they were okay.

They waved goodbye from the stoop of their home, with their two dogs by their side. I waved back and shook my head in disbelief. This couple had seen the worst Mother Nature could hand out and still their faith was not shaken. They had provided me with renewed strength and resolve to carry on and I thanked God for their encouragement.

Chapter Fourteen—Our Homes Were Simply Swept Away

Freeport, The Bahamas

November 2019

It was three months after Hurricane Dorian made landfall on the island of Grand Bahamas, doing its best to destroy this island paradise.

Grand Bahama is the jewel of the country, with endless white sand beaches and spectacular coral reefs that invite swimmers into their snorkeling paradise. The bustling town of Freeport has something for everyone from five-star resorts to family-owned restaurants that serve the islands' signature conch meals. Dorian brought everything to a halt.

Grand Bahamas' once-beautiful pine forests were totally destroyed by Hurricane Dorian.

Dorian was tracking to the south of Grand Bahamas and it looked like the island might be spared the worst of the storm. Then it made a surprise right turn and crossed over the island to the shallower, northern offshore waters. Those shallower waters to the north of the island intensified the tremendous storm surge that was more than two stories tall when it reached landfall. It nearly inundated the entire island.

Grand Bahamas is more than four miles wide along the eastern end and the storm surge pushed inland until it reached the ridge running down the middle of the island. Then the water raced down the back side of the ridge in a torrent of water and debris. The surge hit the homes along the southern edge of the island and simply swept them, and the families inside them, out into the sea. Never to be seen again. This was especially troublesome to Bahamians, who view the custom of burying their dead with high importance.

The devastation was like none I had ever seen during my previous disaster responses.

The homes along this beach road were simply swept out to sea by the storm surge caused by Hurricane Dorian.

I was working with a team of government engineers assessing the damage on the east end of the island. The reconstruction efforts still seemed overwhelming even three months after the event. Critical utilities such as electricity and water service were still months away from being restored, and many of the damaged homes remained in their collapsed state. Debris was everywhere, still requiring frequent stops to cut a path with a chainsaw to access and assess the damage. Even the groundwater had been contaminated by the twenty-foot-high storm surge of sea water that had percolated through the soil, giving the drinking water a strong salty taste that could last for more than a year.

I expressed my doubt to my colleague that this portion of the island would ever be rebuilt. But he pointed out that progress was being made. If we only looked for it.

Some roadways had been cleared, and homeowners had started to pile up the debris. Tents had been provided by Rotary to the residents so they could camp out in their front yards while they worked on their homes. Temporary drinking water stations were also established by Rotary at the end of the streets so people could fetch clean, fresh water. People were working and chatting with each other and it seemed everyone now had a plan on how to rebuild their lives.

I had forgotten the neatly-packed lunch back on my bed, and my stomach was urging me to seek out some food, when I spotted a restaurant at the end of the road. The faded blue building was small and clearly had been severely damaged. But the yard had been cleared, the debris removed, and repairs were well underway. A sign hung on the wall indicating that the site was being used as an emergency food distribution site for the community.

*Tents provided temporary shelter while people restored
their homes after Hurricane Dorian.*

The restaurant was abuzz with volunteers working on needed repairs. The roof had been replaced along with a new floor, and interior repairs were well underway. Other building owners had started their repairs, but this restaurant clearly led the way with its swift progress. Joshua, the owner, greeted me with a firm handshake and a smile while he wiped the sweat from his brow. He was tall, athletic, and dressed in old, blue coveralls with a New York Yankees baseball cap perched on his head.

"Sorry, no fresh meal to eat in this town—but I can offer you one of these military Meals Ready to Eat (MRE's). We have a ton of them. If you come back in a month, I would be happy to serve you the best seafood lunch you have ever had," he said with a smile.

He showed me around the property, gave me an MRE, and we sat down on a couple of rocks looking over the ocean.

He told me his storm story and how he and his family had left their home for higher ground when the warnings came but were still forced to take refuge on a rooftop as the water rose twenty feet from the sea surge.

"We have all seen terrible hurricanes before. But we had never seen anything close to this. It was incredibly frightening. All we could do is pray that God would stop the water from rising up to us," he said.

After the storm surge retreated, he returned to his home to find that the sea had swept away three members of his extended family.

He looked toward the ocean and said, "I never saw them again."

We sat in silence looking across the blue sea, letting the sun wash across our faces. It was unimaginable that such a beautiful scene could have turned so ugly.

"But we must move on. Look at the progress we have made!" He beamed and waved his hand at the restaurant. "I started to do the work by myself but soon the everyone joined in. We all want to get the restaurant open as a sure sign of progress for the entire neighborhood."

I asked him where he gets his strength and he said, "God has given me life and these amazing friends. We must rebuild and be a symbol of hope. It is like the song, *This little light of mine, I'm going to let it shine.*"

He started to sing the song in his loud, booming voice. At this point, all the volunteers joined in a rousing rendition, dancing and singing as they worked. As they continued to sing, I joined in and the feeling of hope washed over me.

I said goodbye to Joshua and his friends. I thought how

important his positive attitude was to his community and how it must have given them all hope and inspiration. What a powerful message that even in adversity, letting one's "little light shine" can inspire and give hope to those around us. Sometimes it just takes one person to light the way.

Mozambique

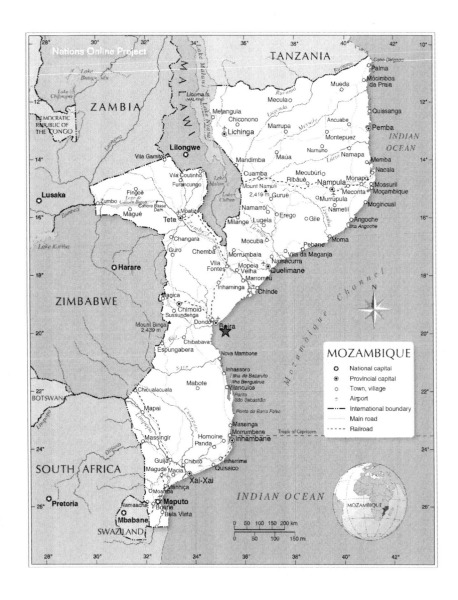

MOZAMBIQUE

- ⊙ National capital
- ⊙ Provincial capital
- ○ Town, village
- ⊼ Airport
- —— International boundary
- ········· Main road
- - - - Railroad

Chapter Fifteen—Living on a Roof for Ten Days

Beira, Mozambique

June 2019

Living on a roof for ten days was the reality that the people of Buzi, Mozambique found themselves in after Cyclones Idai and Kenneth hit the country in March and April 2019. The category four storms slammed into their country and relentlessly pounded them for hours with wind and rain.

The people of Buzi taking refuge on their roofs.
(Photo courtesy of the Mozambique Ministry of Reconstruction)

Mozambique was vulnerable even before the storms, being the ninth poorest country on the planet, based upon the Human Development Index. The cyclones certainly did not help. First, their strong winds completely destroyed the traditional homes built of stick and mud and blew off most roofs of even the strongest homes. Then, as the rains continued and the river rose, the people found their homes flooded by up to six feet of water. The floods stretched as far as the eye could see in this flat coastal terrain.

Their only refuge was any remaining roof that could support them. Family after family was forced from their home, then waded to the few remaining intact roofs at the center of town to join their neighbors. The rains continued to pelt them on the roofs, and they feared what might happen if the roofs were submerged or collapsed. After the storm subsided, the waters continued to rise as the days passed and the sun now baked them. Space on the roofs was limited and they had to take turns standing so that others could sit down to rest or sleep. Day after day, they stayed on the roofs with no food or clean water, always wondering when, or if, the waters would recede.

I was there as part of an engineering team to assist the United Nations and the Government of Mozambique in response to the disaster. We were working to repair the schools and clinics as quickly as possible. We were also tasked with providing temporary shelter and rebuilding houses for those who had lost everything. The work seemed endless.

The public buildings had all been flooded, including the hospital. This forced doctors, nurses, and patients to retreat to bleachers at the soccer field, where they set up a temporary hospital without even a tarp for a roof. This is a move no

The temporary hospital at the soccer stadium during the ten days of flooding. (Photo courtesy of the Mozambique Ministry of Reconstruction)

doctor wants to make, but they had no choice as building after building on the hospital grounds was flooded. One pregnant woman even gave birth at the soccer stadium lying on a bench.

I asked the director of the hospital how she managed to provide health care under such conditions. She looked away, overcome by emotion as she remembered those terrible days. Then she turned and looked me square in the eye and said, "You do what you have to do."

*The makeshift hospital in Buzi after the
flooding destroyed the buildings.*

In Buzi, the entire city had been flooded. The Government
had made the decision to relocate the city of 25,000 people who
lived within the flood plain to safer ground twenty miles away.
It was a difficult decision, but the threat of increased storms due
to climate change made reconstructing the town within the
flood plain a poor choice. Another, safer location was needed.

The engineering challenges of rebuilding a city were
daunting as we worked to build new schools, hospitals,
roads, and utilities. But the social issues of moving an entire
community were even more of a challenge. How do you move
people who have been living in one place for generations?

These people had lost everything and now needed to move to a strange place twenty miles away, hoping to start a new life. As I visited with one homeowner who was packing up what few possessions survived the storm, I asked her how she felt about leaving her home.

She told me her mother was very upset. Her mother did not want to leave because she had lived her whole life at the family home and had many fond memories. But her daughter told me the mother was also concerned that climate change would bring additional storms and felt blessed to have a safe place to move.

The woman told me, "We will rebuild our lives on higher ground that won't flood the next time the cyclones come. Sure, the walls and roof of our building were destroyed, but our home is still intact. We all survived the storm, and our home is here," as she rested her hand on her heart.

"Our whole neighborhood is moving, so we will not be alone," she said, now managing a smile and nodding to her neighbors. "Our community is strong, and we will support each other. I just hope we can all build our new homes next to each other to re-establish the same neighborhood." I reassured her that we would have building lots for her and her neighbors all located together in the new community.

I looked at her standing in the debris of what had been her home. There was nothing left, not even a pot to boil water. How could this woman be so strong in the face of such adversity? She reached down into the rubble and pulled up a broken cross. She calmly wiped the mud from the cross and straightened it before carefully placing it in her pocket.

"God has taken care of us during the storm," she said. "He will watch over all of us and help us rebuild."

What's left of a simple home flooded by the storm.

I was humbled by her faith, knowing that mine would waiver in the face of such adversity. So many times, we prize the physical possessions of our home or church. We fail to think beyond the physical walls and roof of the building. If we lose our physical possessions, we think we have lost everything.

This woman had taught me the lesson that the building is not important. It is the people who fill the building that really matter. When God's people stick together and support each other as a community, even the most daunting challenge may be overcome.

Philippines

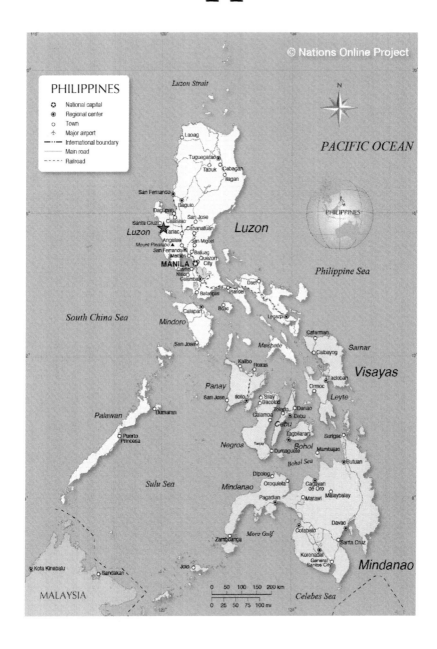

Chapter Sixteen—Judgment

Luzon, Philippines

April 2015

My flight arrived in Manila at midnight, and I decided to sleep in the airconditioned airport for a few hours before catching a 5:00 am bus to the project site. A big mistake. The bus station was less than two miles from the airport, and I thought I had reserved plenty of time when I flagged down a taxi to take me the short distance at 3:00 am—a full two hours before the bus would depart.

Riding inside a Filipino jeepney or taxi can be an adventure.

The taxi driver winced when I told him my destination and that I had a 5:00 am bus to catch. "I doubt that we will make it in time. Traffic is crazy all night long here in Manila," he said.

He was right. I missed my bus and scrambled to catch the next one to the site.

The traffic might be crazy, but the Philippines is a beautiful country with wonderfully friendly people. The contrast between the urban life in Manila and the countryside is striking; even a few hours from the city, the farmers live a very different lifestyle.

The countryside near the project site, with the ocean in the background.

I was volunteering to assist the Army Corp of Engineers of the Philippines and the US Navy Seabees on the Philippine island of Luzon. The joint building mission was to construct three pedestrian bridges that would allow farming families to get to markets and services.

At the first bridge site, I quickly made friends with Maria, one of the members of the town council. She was referred to as the "Mother of Engineers" because she often boarded marine engineering students studying at a nearby university. Maria is a happy and pleasant woman who lives with her husband and three dogs that she pampers like children. She loves to cook and was happy to prepare a homemade lunch each day during the assignment, a welcome substitute for military MREs (Meals Ready to Eat). We soon become good friends.

Maria, her husband, and their three dogs.

Unlike other projects I have worked on, this joint military operation engaged the community cautiously and on a limited basis. The offer by local residents to help with the bridge construction was flatly rejected with little explanation. "We just wanted to help and be part of the project. No need to be rude," A community member told the lieutenant.

In fact, the community members were allowed near the site and an armed guard was posted to prevent anyone from even checking on the progress of the work each evening.

When the locals asked if they might use the Army's truck to haul away some debris at the school, the lieutenant said no immediately, leaving the people scratching their heads as they looked at the idle truck parked under a tree.

I was getting frustrated with this different delivery model that had no community engagement or input. Materials were delivered from hours away when local stores offered the same items at a much lower price. When I arranged a meeting with the local store owners and the quartermaster to discuss how they might be able to participate in the procurement process, the lieutenant quickly dismissed the idea and scolded me for wasting his time.

"You made me look bad today, Engineer. Don't you ever do that again," he said in a commanding voice.

The military chain of command was also new to me. I was not allowed to talk with the other soldiers while on the project site. Any construction suggestion or quality concern had to be addressed to the appropriate soldier who would then pass it up the chain of command.

I puzzled over the situation as I poked at one of Maria's tasty lunches that included local and very different dishes.

"What's wrong, Engineer? Do you not like Filipino food?" she asked.

I explained my frustration to her. She smiled at me as she heaped another spoonful of food on my plate and asked me to not pass judgment on the lieutenant.

"Remember Romans 14:13," she said. "Let us not pass judgment on one another."

One of Maria's lunches fit for a king.
When we sat down and gave thanks for our food, she said this prayer:
"And Father, please give peace to the hearts of the soldiers and
understanding to the engineer."

I was shocked. Why was this woman so understanding when the lieutenant had been so rude to her and her community?

Then one night while the soldiers wrote letters home, I heard them talking about their experiences in Afghanistan. Many of the soldiers from the Seabees unit had recently spent considerable time in Afghanistan. They talked about their friends who had been killed and maimed during the war. They also talked about how many of the local people were punished by the enemy for even talking to them. I got chills down my spine from their stories of finding the local villagers mutilated bodies as a message to the rest of the community to not cooperate with the soldiers.

I relayed the story to Maria at our next lunch and she smiled back at me. "It sounds like God answered my prayer. He let you hear these stories so you would understand why the lieutenant acts the way he does," she said while placing one final scoop of food on my plate.

As the weeks wore on, the soldiers and I worked together as a team. I now understood their approach was to protect each other and the community around them. As our mission ended, one of the soldiers gave me a bandana with the ninety-first Psalm written on it. It is known as "The Soldier's Prayer" and the psalm ends with:

"I will be with him in trouble. I will deliver him and honor him. With long life I will satisfy him and show him my salvation."

I thank Maria for showing me how to open my heart to understanding and empathy instead of judgment.

The joint military crew from the US Navy Seabees and the Army Corp of Engineers of the Philippines at the bridge construction site.

Chapter Seventeen, Eighteen, Nineteen, and Twenty Locations
Guatemala

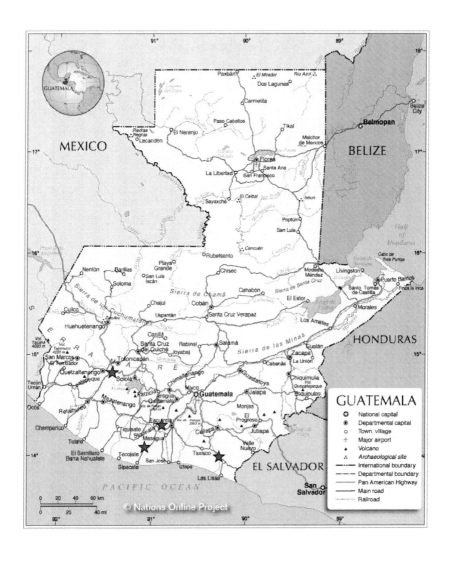

Chapter Seventeen—Healing Together

Rio Cenizas, Guatemala

November 2018

I looked up from the base of the smoldering Volcano Fuego in Guatemala that had erupted six months earlier in June 2018 and tried to imagine that fateful day. We were working as part of the Guatemalan Government's disaster response. Our mission was to rebuild bridges that would restore critical evacuation routes for communities at risk during future eruptions. Without the bridges, these people are trapped without a way to reach safety. They are forced to live in constant fear of another eruption.

The community of Rio Cenizas has fifteen thousand people who live close to the volcano and suffered terribly during the eruption, which occurred around noon and started with very loud explosions. The people looked up to see the boiling cloud of ash and debris flowing down the volcano toward their homes and families. They quickly ran back from their fields to their houses, seeking shelter with their family. As they sat inside their homes, they could hear the larger stones hit their roofs and the blast of wind tug at the roofing sheeting. Finer material came through small cracks around the doors and windows, filling the rooms with ash, as if they were full of smoke. Everyone soon was coughing and gasping to breathe while wondering what might be next.

June 3, 2018
Volcano Fuego eruption.

This was my seventh disaster response, and I saw a similar effect on the community as I'd seen caused by other disasters. The social fabric is stretched and torn as people lose confidence in their God, leaders, neighbors, and sometimes even their families. During and immediately after the event, people wonder why their friends and families did not come to their aid.

"Where was everyone during my time of need?" they would ask themselves and neighbors.

In the days that follow the event, time moves very slowly, and people start to wonder if their leaders and government have abandoned them.

"Don't they know we are suffering? Where are they? Have they given up on us?"

Then, as they bury the dead and the full impact of the disaster is understood and felt, people begin to even question their God.

"How can God allow such an event to occur that causes such suffering?"

The local pastor explained that the people's fear eventually turned to sadness and anger as they worked to recover from the eruption. This had been a happy community with a strong faith before the event, but that had changed. Attendance was down at the church and he struggled to find answers for the questions that were being asked of him. Did God really exist?

The bridge project needed to engage a large number of stakeholders if it were to succeed. It included eight communities, two regional governments and the Army, which was leading the response for the Guatemalan federal government. Each had an important role to play, and all doubted that the other partners would do their part.

Nobody trusted each other. Many were sure the project would fail. They feared that they lacked the ability to control their own destiny and had to rely on the other groups for success—the very same people who they felt had abandoned them in their time of need.

We began the bridge construction with a workforce of one hundred strong, but reluctant, volunteers. The groups worked on their respective tasks, but doubt remained, and energy was low. Many felt they were wasting their time. They would not allow themselves to believe that the important bridge that would provide the evacuation route to safety would be completed. The work seemed to be too much for even so many hands to accomplish. I began to wonder if we would have the workers to complete the bridge, because fewer and fewer workers showed up each day.

As the bridge slowly took shape, the working groups started to interact more. Mother Nature was also hard at work as the fresh green shoots of growth started to peek through the gray, dusty ash. The mood improved and the chatter became livelier. How is your mother doing in the hospital? Has your home been repaired yet?

Something positive was finally happening in the lives of the community. The new bridge would be bigger, stronger, and more beautiful than the previous one that was destroyed. Now, people wanted to be part of the project and its positive energy. The volunteer work teams grew as excitement built. We struggled to keep them all busy on meaningful work.

Soon "random acts of kindness" started to occur. Women came and prepared hot, fresh Guatemalan coffee for the workers. Bunches of bananas and baskets of mangoes were

Plants begin to grow after the eruption,
as the volcano smoldered in the background.

122

dropped off by people in passing vehicles as they urged the workers on with a "thumbs up" and honks from their horns. Smiles were replacing frowns.

Finally, the day came when heavy cables needed to be pulled across the river. One hundred and three souls toiled together to move the six thousand pounds of cable—a task that would be impossible if everyone did not work together. As the people picked up the cable and pulled together, it slowly moved like a centipede with two hundred and six legs. As the workers grunted and strained together under the hot sun with sweat dripping off the ends of their noses, old friendships were renewed, and the social fabric began to mend. They were becoming a community once again.

A volunteer roasts fresh coffee beans in a "Random act of kindness."

A few weeks later, it was Sunday, and I was leaving. The bridge was completed. I smiled as I saw the church now overflowing with attendees spilling out the front door and I heard people singing songs of praise. I realized that this project was more than building an important bridge—it was about helping bring healing to a community that had been through so much.

Sometimes we need someone else to show us the positive things in our lives after our own personal disaster. Healing takes time and patience, but God is always there, never frustrated with us. He uses each of us to help others in our own way. Sometimes a smile, a simple greeting or conversation at the right time is what is needed to help someone mend the fabric of a troubled life. The Lord works in mysterious ways and sometimes amazing things happen when we allow him to use us as instruments in his hands.

*The completed bridge with Volcano Fuego
smoldering in the background.*

Chapter Eighteen—A Christmas Present at Socorro

Socorro, Guatemala

December 2018

As the engineering team made its way to the project site, we passed El Rodeo—a grim reminder of our work. The community had been completely destroyed by Volcano Fuego's June 3, 2018 eruption that buried the homes in hot ash, boulders and debris, killing many of its residents. The roadway had been cleared, but I felt sad looking at the once-thriving, happy community that now lay in silent ruins as we drove by.

Volcano Fuego with the lahars scaring its face.

We arrived in Socorro, a community that is in the heart of sugar cane country and approximately twenty miles from the volcano. It was six months after the main eruption, but the event was still fresh in everyone's memory.

The people in this rural farming community make a living by chopping cane in near one-hundred-degree humid weather. After I was there a few days, the people opened up to me about the fateful night of the eruption. I was reminded of the lyrics *"Does anyone know where the love of God goes, when the events change the minutes to hours."*

They told of the loud explosions and the ground shaking from the destructive mudflow called a lahar, flowing in the river. This was not new to them. The community had been heavily damaged fifty-four years earlier when the volcano erupted, lahar filled the river with ash debris and pushed the river into their homes. That event killed several members of the community and its story had been shared with family members over the years. They told me they again felt afraid as memories came flooding back.

After the initial blast of the eruption, they left their homes to inspect the damage. The people gathered on the banks of the river and watched the lahar flow and turn their once clean, friendly stream into an ugly and threatening foe—killing all the fish and vegetation that once thrived within its banks. The lahar was so hot that it burned anyone who dared to touch it. Soon the footbridge over the river was overcome and destroyed—eliminating this important evacuation route to safety.

The community was now isolated. They could not escape, and help could no longer reach them. This is what brought me and the Rotary engineering team to this community.

We were there to replace the bridge and the connection for the people to education, markets, healthcare—and most importantly—safety.

The ground continued to shake with minor eruptions, and nobody knew if additional, even more powerful events loomed in the future. Some families sent the women and children away after the eruption to stay with other family members out of fear for their safety during future eruptions. But many stayed in their homes, tended their fields and accepted the risk of living without a safe evacuation route to cross the river. This was their home, and they had no place else to go.

Maria is a proud and strong grandmother who sells tortillas three times a day to make a living. Her little shop was positioned near the old bridge crossing and the smell of fresh tortillas soon caught my attention. I pulled up a stool to enjoy some, and she told the story of how she misjudged the river just a week before my arrival, when she attempted to wade across the river with her grandson.

As they reached the river's strongest current, the water swept the legs out from under her little grandson and she knew they were in trouble. She hung onto both of his hands. His legs stretched out downstream as the current tugged at them. He never said a word, or even cried—but looked at her knowing that she was the only thing between life and death. As her grip on her grandson's little hands started to wane, Maria cried out for help. Luckily, two men heard her and came to their rescue. She wiped the tears from her leathery cheek and proud face as she trembled—undoubtedly thinking what might have happened.

As we worked on the new bridge, the landscape sent us a constant message of the volcano's presence. We could see five volcanos from the site—Fuego, Acatenango, Agua, Pacaya and Atitlan. Fuego had minor eruptions several times a day, sending a plume of ash high up into the sky. Sometimes, the eruptions were more serious and demanded our attention with their loud explosions. Try as I might, I could not help but wonder if the "Big One" was yet to come.

It was cane harvesting time in the area. The fields are first burned and then the cane is chopped by the workers, stacked and put into large trucks to be taken to the sugar mill. When the fields are burned, iguanas flee and local people pounce on them like cats. Iguana is a welcome source of protein for families there and we were no different. Our reliable cook made a wonderful stew, or "caldo de iguana."

The cane harvest went on seven days a week without pause. This made it difficult to find forty men needed to volunteer to work on bridge construction. After several attempts to find new recruits, we called a community meeting to discuss this challenge.

Most people talked about how the task was impossible. I could feel the frustration growing. Then, Audrey, the leader from Socorro, asked if women might be able to help. Mincho, our construction foreman immediately said "yes," and that we would work side by side with them (it is extremely rare for us to have women workers on construction sites in Guatemala). So, the next morning at 6:30 am, twenty-five mothers and grandmothers, many with children in tow, came to work.

They worked tirelessly, carrying rocks the size of volleyballs along with mixing and carrying concrete. Doing this work is a challenge for even an hour or two, but these ladies kept up the pace all morning. Just when I thought that they must give out, Audrey started to sing a Christmas hymn and the rest of the group all joined in, now with renewed energy. Inspired by these amazing women, the following morning twenty-five teenage girls also came ready to pitch in. They were eager to show their fathers, brothers, and boyfriends that they too could do a day's work.

A week later, I was amazed as I watched the labor, which now progressed rapidly. The women were always socializing— talking about their families, complaining about their men and urging each other on.

The proud women of Socorro at the ribbon cutting.

Excitement grew as the bridge took shape—first the tall towers were done, followed by cables and suspenders that would form the deck. Each evening, a crowd gathered at the site to track the progress of the work. I watched as the women workers proudly pointed and waved at the bridge, showing their men the day's progress.

When we started construction in November, we set the goal of having the new bridge as a community Christmas present. Many scoffed, saying it couldn't be done. Now the ladies waited impatiently for me to finish the fencing so they could place the last concrete on the ramp up to the bridge. As the bridge was completed a few days before Christmas, tears of joy and prayers of thanks now flowed because safe passage over the river was again a reality. Soon, Maria came to thank me for our help—only to be unable to utter a word due to emotion. As we hugged instead, I knew no further words were needed.

As I looked at the bridge, I remembered Audrey's courage and determination at the community meeting and how it made all the difference in the project. She did not look outside for help to the problem—but within. She did not fear the construction work, but knew that with God's help, all things are possible. She tackled the impossible task with a hymn on her lips, joy in her heart and never a complaint. She put her faith in God and simply said, "Here I am God, send me."

What a wonderful lesson and gift she had given me that Christmas.

A new bridge is born in the dawn at Socorro.

Chapter Nineteen—Having Faith Can Be Hard

Chiquimulilla, Guatemala

January 2019

Just like every life, every project has its challenges. But this bridge never seemed to catch a break.

It all started nine years ago in 2010 when the bridge that served eight communities in rural Guatemala was destroyed by hurricane Agatha. Immediately, the community started to seek help for a replacement bridge over the river that isolated the people for five months during the rainy season. Time and again, the government or other groups would come and assess a new bridge crossing, but the answer was always the same. A new bridge was impossible.

When I visited the bridge site for the first time in July, I could see why nobody wanted to take on the project. The length of three hundred and sixty feet was more than a football field (with the endzones) and one bank of the river was nearly four stories (thirty-five feet) higher than the other. We scoured the terrain up and down the river for a more suitable crossing only to realize that nothing better existed. This would be one of the more challenging sites I had worked on in my thirty years as a civil engineer.

But the need could not be denied—the river was a barrier that prevented the communities from accessing health care, education, and markets. We met with many groups; passionate stories flowed. Several men had lost their lives trying to cross the river, leaving behind widows and children. During just the previous year, four babies and three mothers had died during childbirth because they were unable to get to the hospital. I could see the sadness in the eyes of the people as each story brought back painful memories.

Even after we had agreed to accept the project, the struggles continued. The land on one side of the river was owned by an absentee landowner who would prove to be difficult to find. We needed his right of way permission. One of the donors would not follow through on its promise of funding, leaving what seemed to be an impossible financial gap.

As we started construction, the project's struggles continued. The backhoe from the municipality broke down on the first day, never to be fixed again—leaving excavations that contained boulders the size of cars, impossible to move by hand. The port authority that was donating cable used by its container cranes changed its policy and would no longer be able to make the donation. I became more and more frustrated as the project's challenges continued to pile up.

Octaviano was the organizer of the eight communities and the person who had tirelessly worked to get the bridge replaced. Providing access to his community is "in his blood." He worked as a boy with his father, who led the people in building their eleven-kilometer roadway by using picks and shovels. The project took sixteen years.

Octaviano is a born leader who always wears a smile and

A portion of the community roadway built by hand over sixteen years.

is optimistic. His positive attitude and friendly disposition naturally draw people to him. The man seems like he has never had a bad day; impossible to get him to say anything negative about anything or anyone. He told me that when he was young, the other students made fun of him, saying "You are too cheerful—can't you be normal?"

But clearly, he's not normal. He rose each morning at 4:00 am, did his chores in the dark, and then made the two-hour walk from his house to the bridge site. He constantly encouraged the eight communities and organized the thirty volunteers needed to do the work each day, seven days a week. When I talked with his wife, she said she knows he sometimes worries, but he never allows this to cloud his sunny disposition.

"I guess that is why I love him so much," she said with a broad smile.

The community's leader Octaviano who never lets a smile leave his face.
(Photo Credit: Judy Haselhoef)

As struggles continued to pile up, I began to feel overwhelmed. It seemed the challenges were beyond our abilities to solve and the project would fail. Octaviano could see my despair and asked if I might sit with him under a large tree next to the river. As we settled and I drew in a deep breath, he talked with me about my concerns. He asked me to pray with him. He gave thanks, asking that God's will be done. He asked God to keep the workers safe. He did not ask for any other help with the bridge, putting his faith entirely in God's hands.

He encouraged me to move forward despite my doubts. He reminded me of the story of Jesus feeding the five thousand with only two fish and five loaves of bread. He smiled at me and asked me to have faith. I looked at this man who has so little and wondered where his faith comes from. His simple home had no electricity or water. He had seven chickens three rocky acres of land where he grew the corn and beans that feeds his family. How could this man be so happy and have so much faith with so little—while I struggled with my doubts?

Then things started to break the project's way. Octaviano's friend in the city offered his backhoe, which made quick work of the large boulders. The port authority reconsidered, and we received two used cables from their cranes. After a complete inspection, we determined they were in good condition and could be used for the bridge. Workers began to come in droves and the progress on the bridge began moving at an amazing pace.

A simple home in the community.

Nary was a worker who showed incredible dedication. Each day for more than a month, he rose early in the morning to complete his farming chores before going to the bridge site. There, he used his carpentry expertise to help shape the bridge. He loved learning bridge construction techniques. On Sundays, his entire family gathered at the site and he'd explain his work to his young sons, who beamed with pride in the work of their papa.

When the bridge was finally done, Octaviano came to me with a present. It's a picture of countless small fish drawn by his wife. He smiled as he handed me the picture and asked that I always have faith. I was overcome with emotion as we embraced, knowing that the picture will remind me of my friend and encourage me to always have faith in God.

The completed bridge over the River Los Esclavos.

Chapter Twenty—Struggling at Home

Mukwonago, Wisconsin

April 2020

I found myself struggling with the "Work from Home" model during the COVID-19 pandemic. My international travels to Africa and Central America had been indefinitely postponed. I had so looked forward to the projects—but everything changed with COVID-19's arrival. By early 2021, I'd experienced the longest period that I spent at home in over a decade, and it felt very strange.

But the pandemic demanded that we all contribute in whatever way we could. I found myself doing my best to remotely help hospitals around the globe and right here in Wisconsin to be prepared for the COVID-19 pandemic. This work included increasing the amount of water supplied and stored at hospitals to accommodate the surge in patients. We also built larger waiting rooms, adding toilets and handwashing stations. I found myself in 'disaster mode,' working long hours seven days a week. But this time, the 'disaster control center' was based in my home with countless Zoom meetings.

A new handwashing station at a hospital.

One of the most challenging projects was the work to provide Personal Protective Equipment (PPE) for healthcare workers. A team of biomedical engineer volunteers from Wisconsin universities initially supported manufacturers in the USA to modify their production lines to provide the vital PPE to community hospitals. The biomedical engineers were all connected through previous Engineers Without Borders projects and knew that the struggles in the United States would pale in comparison to those in developing countries. Many had worked in Guatemala on various projects and it soon became clear that vulnerable healthcare facilities were quickly becoming overwhelmed as requests for assistance came pouring in.

The doctors and nurses were doing the best they could without even the most basic PPE to protect themselves from the virus. Many became ill and suffered terribly. The engineering team worked to replicate the local production of PPE in Guatemala by assisting its existing plastics and textile industries to pivot their production to the lifesaving products.

A doctor protected in a locally made gown, mask, and face shield.

There were many challenges working remotely to support hospitals and manufacturers. These include selecting proper materials and manufacturing processes to make a safe and affordable product without being at the manufacturing facility in person. I was leading a call where engineers were brainstorming how they might remotely test the different local fabrics and the assembly processes for medical masks. Guatemala was on a strict lockdown, so transporting samples to a Guatemalan lab was not possible.

Maria is one of the seamstresses who volunteered to lead a group of ladies sewing the medical masks. She is short with long black hair pulled back into a braid that lies softly along her back. Her face always wears a smile, and her eyes seem always to be dancing—even with the rest of her face behind a mask. Like most Guatemalan's, she is quiet by nature, but her soft laugh always seems to raise everyone's spirit.

Guatemalan midwives receiving their PPE.

I had met her a few years back during the implementation of a water project in her village. At the first water meeting, many in her community were confused and concerned. Maria spoke in her quiet and calming voice to the crowd and soon had everyone working together on the job. She is a real leader and people are naturally drawn to her. When she heard about our project to protect her community's healthcare workers with PPE, she immediately reached out and asked how she might help.

She listened intently as the engineers debated on the video call. Different ideas were being considered on how to test the medical mask's ability to stop particles and the virus. The engineers were stumped and frustrated. How could they test the many options quickly without access to the modern equipment? The call ended with the engineers demoralized and they agreed to regroup and brainstorm solutions. Maria said nothing, but I could see that she was thinking behind her mask.

The next day, we all received a message from Maria. It contained a cell phone video of her proposed method to do some initial screening of her ideas. The video showed her blowing at a candle through different medical masks made with varied processes and materials. She could also use the candle's smoke to test the mask's filtration ability. Based upon how the candle's flame reacted, and if she could smell the smoke, she screened her ideas. How simple and elegant! Of course, her final ideas would go through rigorous testing, but her initial screening would prove to be critical for the best medical mask options to be identified and made quickly.

I called Maria to congratulate her on her ingenuity and dedication to the project. She, like all of us, has been working around the clock with little sleep. We talked about the stress, and I shared with her my frustration with the virus—it never stops; it never sleeps; it does not stop for weekends and seems to relentlessly stalk its victims. I confessed to her that I was starting to feel overwhelmed.

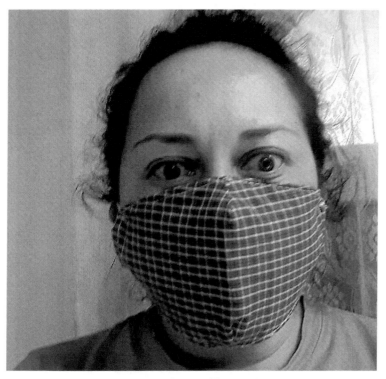

Maria with one of her masks.

"Oh Miguel," she responded. "Yes, the virus is terrible and persistent. But God's love is even more powerful. It never stops; it never sleeps, it does not stop for weekends and it is always there for us. We can all draw our strength from God's love during this time if we simply submit ourselves to his grace."

She asked me to pray with her. She asked God for wisdom and strength—and to lighten the team's hearts by removing our worry and stress. She prayed that God use us all as his instruments during this time of crisis.

"Can I give you a 'virtual hug'? I feel so much better and my heart is now so inspired."

"Why of course," she said in her cheerful voice and trademark laugh.

I somehow felt her strength and encouragement flow through the phone line into my body. I was rejuvenated and ready to continue God's work against the virus.

Once again, my friends have shared important lessons with me. God will take the worry and stress from us if we only allow him. Even though we may be separated by many miles, we can still support and encourage each other during times of crisis.

Acknowledgements

I would like to thank all of those who have shown me their amazing hospitality and shared their wisdom from around the world during my adventures. You always seemed to have the right words or have shared a smile at the right time to lift me up. You truly have been my *Global Inspiration*.

My parents put me on my faith journey at an early age, and I have come to appreciate that this is a luxury that many in this world do not have. It has given me a new appreciation for those who have not grown up in a faith-based family and the need for missions to share God's love. Thank you, Mom and Dad.

Thank you to Shannon and the team at Ten16 Press for sharing my vision for the book and putting up with my 'crazy ideas'. Also, a special thanks to Gail Grenier, who edited the book. It is no small task to edit the words from an engineer and make them fitting for the public.

I would also like to acknowledge Pastor Steve and Kevin Colvett, who helped with the story about Cata—everyone's favorite person who continues to inspire us all every day.

A special thanks to Judy Haselhoef, who has 'the patience of Job' and keeps writing fun. You are an inspiration.

And finally, to my wife of over thirty years, Cathy. She has stuck with this crazy engineer through thick and thin. I can't imagine going through this life without you.

About the Author

Michael Paddock (in photo above with his wife, Cathy, in Guatemala) grew up in Northern Minnesota and attended Michigan Technological University, receiving bachelor's degrees in civil engineering and surveying. He is a licensed professional engineer and surveyor whose professional career at CH2M HILL was spent managing teams of more than 100 engineers designing infrastructure projects exceeding $1 billion. He was the youngest- ever recipient of Wisconsin's "Engineer of the Year" award.

After a near-fatal cancer experience, he was motivated to begin a pro bono engineering career that has led over 100 projects with Engineers Without Borders USA, Rotary and other nonprofits on five continents during the last twenty years. He currently lives in Southeast Wisconsin with his wife Cathy.

In 2020 he published *BRIDGING BARRIERS: How a Community Changed Its Future with Help From Engineers Without Borders USA Volunteers.*